The Canada Crisis

The Canada Crisis

A Christian Perspective

Douglas Hall

WIPF & STOCK · Eugene, Oregon

Wipf and Stock Publishers
199 W 8th Ave, Suite 3
Eugene, OR 97401

The Canada Crisis
A Christian Perspective
By Hall, Douglas John
Copyright©1980 by Hall, Douglas John
ISBN 13: 978-1-5326-7452-5

Publication date 2/1/2019
Previously published by Anglican Book Centre, 1980

for
Kate, Christopher, Sara, and Lucy,
and the "new breed of anglophone
Canadians" among their generation

Contents

Forward to the 2019 Reprint Edition

I TEACH INTRODUCTORY CHRISTIAN theology to undergraduate students at a Canadian public university. I aim to open a space in the imaginations of diverse students for what it might entail—for themselves, for Canada, and for the world—to utilize a worldview which is distinctly biblical and Christian (and, to guide students in making explicit for themselves the pre-theoretical framework of values that had operated implicitly beforehand).

I am delighted, therefore, to retrieve and re-present this volume from Douglas John Hall who began his own undergraduate theological education at Huron University College at Western University in London, Ontario, Canada. But I am also grateful for this project because Hall's work takes seriously the distinctly *Canadian* context of his life-long theological reflections.

Theology should always be contextually grounded. The Gospel of Jesus Christ needs to be articulated for each unique time and place with its dynamism revealed afresh. Hall's *The Canada Crisis* seeks to do just this: to articulate a Christian perspective on both the positive and negative currents at work within Canada's history and culture.

Hall did this at the end of the 1970s, taking into his Christian consciousness the unique opportunities and pitfalls emerging on the Canadian horizon. Conflict between English-speaking and French-speaking Canadians was threatening national unity. But, at the same time, Canada's national identity was being cemented through its newly-granted legislative independence from the British parliament. Hall sought to show where a distinctly Christian *hope* was to be found in the midst of cultural-historical developments that gave the population reasons for both optimism and despair.

This may be one of the strongest reasons why *The Canada Crisis* is important for the rest of North America: because the United States is, today, approaching a similar point of crisis. It is a crisis Europeans already know well from their history throughout the twentieth century. Hall's Christian perspective on the unique contextual challenges within Canada can give American Christians the opportunity to discern for themselves anew where Christian hope can be found—a hope which transcends both shallow, faddish optimism and nihilistic, soul-killing despair. These are currents which are more discernable with each day's news reports.

Some of these same cultural challenges remain for Canada today as well. If one were to listen to the loudest cultural voices in Canada today, one might sense the same "hope versus despair" dialectic that Hall identified almost forty years ago. The polarization runs deep if we consider two contemporary Canadians who have reached the world stage. On the one hand, there is a segment of the Canadian population today that boisterously celebrates the glamorous, youthful, and—thus—hopeful prime-ministership of Justin Trudeau while simultaneously despairing of the phenomenal cultural ascendency of the University of Toronto psychologist, Jordan B. Peterson and his *12 Rules for Life.*

The same "Trudeaumania" surrounded Canada's prime minister in the late 1970s, Pierre Elliot Trudeau (the current prime minister's father), when Hall was giving this set of lectures (1979) and seeing them first published (1980). But whereas the name that gave Canada global recognition back then (the elder Trudeau) was a *political* institution-builder, the names that give Canada its global recognition today (Peterson and the younger Trudeau) facilitate and embody authentic *personal* transformation. Clearly, public opinion varies on such matters in a stunningly diverse population north of thirty-seven million. But something has shifted from the political to the personal. And yet even though there have been changes, the most prominent Canadians on the world stage today are perceived as icon and foil (take your pick) of the same national cultural impulses of hope and despair. These currents run deep in our beautiful landscape.

So while the push and pull of hope and despair continue across the Canadian consciousness (the identification of which gives Hall's work its ongoing contemporaneity for Canadians), we might wonder what specifically has changed socio-culturally in the "true north, strong and free" since *The Canada Crisis* was first published. Hall's fellow faculty member at Montreal's McGill University, Charles Taylor, has identified the cultural shift that began to dawn in the sixteenth century and has come to proud glory in the 21st century as the establishment of "A Secular Age." Around five hundred years ago in Europe, it was nearly impossible to *not* believe in God; today it is nearly impossible *to* believe in God.

But, in particular, it is Taylor's identification of the "Age of Authenticity" and its concomitant cultural polarizations that have marred our common cultural landscape and ushered in a new dynamic to the hope and despair we feel today in Canada. In the "Age of Authenticity," each person is believed to have an inherent and inalienable right to define for themselves what it means to be human. What this means is that while older generations seek what is true, younger generations today are searching for what is "true for me." A half century ago, the Canadian consciousness was geared toward an external, objective goal (stitching a nation together). Today, a growing segment of the younger population is seeking an internal, subjective goal (expressions of personal authenticity). And because the variables along the whole range of human dimensionality lead us to an infinite number of personal differences, one wonders today if there is a centre, much less whether it will be able to hold us together or not.

Thus, while Hall originally wrote out of a sense of crisis (as a positive and negative potentiality) and observed that "the language of crisis is neither familiar nor palatable to most Canadians"

(17), it is no less palatable today but existentially evermore present in its familiarity. The deep awareness of perennial un- or under-employment, rampant mental illness and suicide, intractable historical and ongoing forms of injustice, institutionalized forms of abuse and discrimination, and the growing number of ever-more-militant protest movements (all conceived either locally or globally) render the Canadian consciousness prone to extended bouts of deeper and deeper despair.

What antidotes could Canadian Christians contribute from their own theological reflections in light of this intractable sense of crisis? From where might we recover our sense of Christian hope in a continually evolving Canada? I still find personal encouragement and practical direction from Hall's three imperatives outlined in this text. I find them to be theologically sound, culturally insightful, and deeply in tune with the missional nature of biblical Christian faith.

First, Canadian Christians must reflect, probably more deeply than they may have in the past, on their discipleship as also encompassing their citizenship. Without falling into the heresy of nationalism which Hall rightly identifies in these pages, Christians seeking to follow the Lord Jesus Christ in Canada today are called to steward their nation out of a distinctly Christian ethic of compassion, care, and justice. This ethic eschews a "my country, right or wrong" attitude with public forms of service that display God's call to each of us to use our gifts, skills, and opportunities for the flourishing of our land (a penultimate goal) so that it might be equipped and stimulated to promote the flourishing of all lands within God's Creation (the ultimate goal). In this extended period of crisis, Canadian Christians need to be reminded that it is God's nature to bless (penultimate goal) in order that the divine blessing might be shared with others (ultimate goal), not bottled up and kept privately for one's self. Like the manna of old, God's blessings have a "best before" date. If they are stored away, out of a desire for personal or tribal security, they poison rather than nourish.

Second, extending God's blessings to others will invariably take the shape of tangible/practical forms of love for our neighbour—and even our (political, ideological, etc) enemy (Matthew 5:43). Hall recognized that there is often something distressingly *theoretical* about many expressions of Christian love: to affirm one's love of all people too often results in a failure to actually love the other who lives next door (and who, after all, irritates us to no end). Many practical theologians today would call this the missional nature of Christian love: it seeks out the other, encounters the other in our common humanity, and serves the other in self-sacrificial and long-suffering forms of love. Middle-class Canadian Christians, comfortable in their secluded neighbourhoods, might be shocked to discover the tangible forms of brokenness in their neighbour's lives, their neighbourhood as an inter-connected community, and even their municipality as a legal entity. There is much love needed in a Canada still stressed along many seams if the fabric of our national identity is to continue to be a welcoming place for the aboriginal, immigrant, and refugee within our political jurisdiction. As the Christian saints have discovered long before us, it might just be through our reaching out to others in need that we discover our own need and find our need met through an encounter with the Other.

Finally, and possibly most significantly for today, Canadian Christians need to realize that Christendom has finally collapsed under its own weight. The Christian Scriptures no longer provide the moral framework within which Canadians understand and live their lives. The Christian Church is no longer chaplain to the country's moral conscience. But this is not something to be lamented as Christians often impulsively feel. For, inherent within a Christendom worldview are forms of institutional and cultural power that are deeply foreign to the Christian Gospel and scriptures. Instead, this new pluralist reality ought to be embraced—even celebrated—by Canadian Christians. Our newly displaced, marginal social location means that we can again constructively engage with our diverse world in a theologically non-triumphalist and ecclesially non-imperialist manner, reaching toward a mutually-discerned common good through horizontal partnerships rather than hierarchical imposition. Maybe by being shoved to the cultural margins, Canadian Christians will be able to re-imagine their vocation to serve, bless, and love with fresh vigor, fruit borne from a new encounter with God's Spirit through faith rather than our technological ingenuity or corporate management.

With these three imperatives in mind, *The Canada Crisis* may, in fact, be a more difficult book to read in 2019 than it was in 1980. The cultural challenges are more entrenched now and thus we must unshackle our imaginations to an even greater degree. We must trace Hall's lines of thought and then extend their trajectories to our lived realities today. And, we must do the hard interpretive work in our new day of where true Christian hope lies rather than lazily settling for one or the other of its cheap alternatives (happy-clappy optimism or despairing resignation).

Here lies Hall's great and enduring gift to us as (Canadian) Christians: in this text, we are reminded that the good news is that, despite the despair we feel and in the face of the challenges we face today, Jesus Christ is still at work. The good news is also that despite our best intentions and our mind-bending scientific ability, it is God alone who remains unrelentingly faithful to Creation's purpose and ultimate end. Thus, at ground zero of our collective consciousness, instead of our countenance being marked by the despair that many believe makes abundant sense in light of the "facts" bombarding us, we can be a people of hope through the sheer faithfulness of this God revealed in Jesus Christ.

Michael R. Wagenman, PhD
Reformation Day 2018
Huron University College, Faculty of Theology
Western University
London, Ontario Canada

Foreword

At this time in all the Christian churches, we find the emergence of new theologies that seek to recover the social meaning of the Christian message. In Jesus Christ, God addresses individual believers as well as the societies to which they belong. Since the individualism characteristic of modern society has made us overlook this social meaning, it is imperative, in obedience to the gospel, that we recover this social dimension at the present.

If these social theologies are correct, it is no longer possible to have a universal theology, the same for people everywhere, for rich and poor, for colonizer and colonized, for people at the top and people at the bottom. We used to argue that the gospel addresses man in his or her personal predicament (in his or her sinfulness and despair), and that since this predicament is identical for all people, independently of their cultural heritage and social location, Christian theology transcends historical circumstances: it is universal. Today many theologians argue against this. They claim that the historical circumstances of life, the concrete conditions of social existence, are part and parcel of the human predicament and that, therefore, God's word in Jesus Christ addresses people in their national situation, in their social location, in the conditions defined by their history.

In this book Douglas Hall presents the outline of a Canadian theology. He tries to bring out the social meaning of the gospel for Canadians, to be precise, for English-speaking Canadians. If Christians believe the gospel addresses them only in regard to their private lives, they will respond to the social conflicts in Canada in accordance with purely secular norms or public opinion or the interests of their class. Douglas Hall argues that Jesus Christ makes a difference. Christians will want to perceive their country, its sins and its future possibilities, from a theological perspective. Hall's reasoning is here wholly convincing.

A few years ago, largely through the writings of the French theologian Jacques Ellul, some Christian writers adopted a radical critique of modern society based on a negative evaluation of technology. The ever expanding application of technology to all aspects of society tends to quantify human life, control human relations, interpret politics as social engineering and transform society into a programmed machine. Technological society leads to loss of soul. With the help of this theory, many Christian preachers spelled out God's judgement on industrial society and in this way tried to recover the social meaning of the gospel. While these preachers offered people a higher spiritual freedom in Jesus Christ, they advocated a perception of society that did not generate social involvement or point to practical social policies. The theory that indiscriminately blames technological society is as abstract and non-historical as were the more traditional theologies, for it allows Christians to look away from the concrete conditions of their social existence — for instance, from the conflicts in Canadian society.

Douglas Hall does not run away from the Canadian reality. He is specific, he names concrete events, he risks being controversial. What is the theological point of entry for his realistic look at Canada? How does he relate the responsibility we have for our country to the gospel of Jesus?

Hall argues that modern western society, including Canada, has, until recently at least, been characterized by an endless cultural optimism. People hope that things will get better and better. Even as we are moving into a crisis of the economy, we still entertain the feeling that after a brief interlude of insecurity and conflict, we shall move ahead again toward greater progress and prosperity. Douglas Hall contrasts this cultural optimism with Christian hope. Cultural optimism is blind and unrealistic, while Christian hope is at all times willing to face "the data of despair." Christian hope is willing to look at the forms of injustice and oppression in this country. Since mainstream culture disguises the structured injustices and since the perception of the middle-class is distorted by self-flattery, the way to collective self-knowledge must pass through two painful phases: we must listen to the groups and sections of the country that have been marginalized, and we must turn to sociological science to get a clearer picture of what oppression looks like in Canada. While Hall's lectures remain almost exclusively theological in style and content, he makes room for the entry of sociological data and sociological analysis into the exercise of theology. Without these, we cannot fully grasp the data of despair.

What Hall does not tell us is that his concentration on social justice corresponds to the shift to the left that has taken place in the churches' social teaching over the last decade. In the documents of church councils, episcopal bodies, and ecclesiastical conferences, including the papacy, we find the emergence of the notion of "social sin" and an extended critique of advanced capitalism as an economic system that widens the gap between the rich and the poor, especially between rich and poor nations, and that allows the decisions regarding resources and consumption to pass into the hands of an ever smaller elite. What the churches affirm is a cooperative society based on participation and responsible planning. This is the ecclesiastical background behind Douglas Hall's social theology for Canada.

Yet Hall is more keenly interested in the theological foundation of his perspective on Canada. He asks the question whether the divine promises made in Jesus Christ have implications for human history. In sermons, we often hear that these promises will be fulfilled only in the world to come; their only effect in the present is peace of soul. Yet according to the biblical teaching, God's promises have an impact on history. They reveal God's redemptive presence to man's historical struggle. If this is true, does this make Christian theology into another theory of human progress and thus a legitimation of cultural optimism?

Here Hall introduces an important distinction. He argues that the divine promises do not assure us of progress in history; what they offer us instead is a qualitative transformation of society. What we are to hope for in Canada is not further growth and development along the lines of the competitive, technological consumers' society. It is unfounded and in the long run dangerous for Canadians to long for Florida sun, the imaginary culture of comfort, convenience, pleasure, and athletic health. The Canadian dream, founded on responsible hope, suggests a more modest and simpler form of life, one that can be shared by all Canadians, a life of reflection and personal depth, a life of discipline appropriate to our winter land, and yet transfigured by a new humanism of participation and equality. Through the contrast between the poetic images of "Florida sun" and "winter light," Hall tries to express what is hope for Canada, hope at odds with optimism, hope in the face of the data of despair, hope for human beings in Canada.

God gives birth to the new in the midst of a troubled land. Hall follows here the theology of Paul Tillich. In the midst of the sinful world God is graciously at work, summoning forth new possibilities of redeemed existence. By discerning this divine presence, the church learns in which way it must move forward.

What are the signs of new life in Canada? Hall hears a summons addressed to Anglo-Canada out of the Quebec experience. While North American culture is largely dominated by the quest for a satisfying and successful private life and hence produces indifference to collective concerns, the people of Quebec, through a process of joint affirmation and struggle for identity, have become involved in a collective project. There is life beyond egotism. While this new sense of "peoplehood" raises uncomfortable questions for Canada, Douglas Hall, himself an Anglophone Canadian living in Montreal, refuses to regard this as a disaster. It is for him an extraordinary event, despite the elements of threat, which reveals the possibility of transcending a purely privatistic perception of society. Quebec is a challenge to English-speaking Canada. We should respond, Hall argues, by permitting ourselves to be inspired. We too should transcend the egotism of modernity by struggling for cultural identity, economic independence and national self-affirmation.

What other signs of new life does Hall acknowledge in Canadian history? He mentions two. He points to the opposition to injustice and exploitation in Canada in the history of the labour movement and the various socialist organizations. There the people, marginalized and excluded from power, laid hold of the principles of solidarity and cooperation to struggle for a society defined by wider participation. Voices calling for justice have never been absent in Canada. As another sign of new life Hall points to Canadian literature and art. He tries to show that these writers and artists are sensitive people who sense the forces of dehumanization in society and who, through their artistic imagination, suggest to us alternatives, new types of human being, passages into the future.

Douglas Hall's book represents a new kind of theological literature. It may indicate a widening Christian concern for Canada and its people. It may signal the emergence of a new spirituality of empowerment that makes Christians, together with other socially involved men and women, makers of a cooperative society. Faith is the radical inability to accept the world as it is because it is meant to be different and can be changed.

Gregory Baum

Preface

This is a book about Canada, and its mood is one of hope. If that sounds strange — given *The Canada Crisis* — it is only because we all underestimate the *positive* side of most human crises. To me, a Canada in crisis contains far more to be hopeful about than our hundred odd years of official hope and rhetorical unity!

Of course hope is not to be confused with optimism. Real hope only comes into its own when the "childish category" (Heidegger) of optimism has been found unhelpful. Hope that is worth its salt has to emerge from an ongoing dialogue with the data of despair. The hopeful side of Canada cannot be seen so long as we continue to push the darker side under the carpet (including the carpet of a tired federalism). Consequently I have written the book especially for people who (with my esteemed friend, George Grant) know something about why we should "lament" for Canada today, but are not yet ready to call "the Canadian experiment" a failure. Failures — from a "Christian perspective" — sometimes turn out to have hidden possibilities of renewal.

The book has been written in a non-technical way because, given its purpose, it could hardly be "for scholars only." Nor is it "for Christians only." For one thing, nothing really Christian is ever "for Christians only." For another, part of Canada's reality is bound up with its religious dimension, and that means mainly Christianity — or a sort thereof. Any resolution of "the

Canada crisis" must involve a re-thinking of that dimension.

The study began as lectures for the twenty-fifth annual Conference of the Theological Students of Canada, meeting in Montréal in February 1979. The students had asked me to speak on the subject "Sin and Hope in Canadian Society."

I am grateful to Gregory Baum, my friend and fellow lecturer on that occasion, for encouraging me to publish the thought of the lectures; to Professor Dick Allen of McMaster University, who seconded the motion; and to the Anglican Book Centre for inviting me to do so. I also want publicly to express my lasting gratitude to Bob Miller, who began these student conferences long ago and who helped a whole generation of us to become aware of our world in crisis. As always I am indebted mostly to my wife Rhoda, with whom over the past twenty years I have been discovering what it really means to be a Canadian and a Christian.

Douglas Hall

Introduction

Turning Point

The official rhetoric of an earlier period would certainly have required the word *challenge:* "Canada is facing an enormous challenge . . ." But when the Task Force on Canadian Unity made its report in January 1979, its key word was not *challenge* but *crisis:* "Canada and its constitutional system is in a protracted state of crisis." The crisis is neither peripheral nor temporary. It lies at the centre of our life as a people, and it will not go away by itself. "Canada is passing through a period of travail which is more than a crisis of development; *it is a crisis of existence itself.* "[1]

The language of crisis is neither familiar nor palatable to most Canadians. It seems extravagant. We are used to such language being applied to "unstable" societies in other parts of the world — Latin America or the Middle East. We are even ready to hear it applied to our great neighbour to the south, whose President recently made official, so to speak, the "crisis of confidence" to which American scholars have been pointing for decades. But we find it strange and uncomfortable when *crisis* is used to describe our own society. Especially when it is put forward as the diagnosis of an officially appointed government commission. More especially still when the crisis the commission depicts is one which pervades our whole society and cannot be laid at the doorstep of any particular guilty segment (the French, Bay Street, Western oil producers).

There are good historical reasons why we dislike the idea of a Canadian crisis. Part of the task of this study will be to explore those reasons. But since I have chosen to discuss our present situation under the nomenclature of crisis, it is only fair that I offer some explanation at the outset of the way in which I should like my readers to hear this word.[2]

On the whole, I think most of us tend to hear only one side of what is contained in the word *crisis*. If we are told that a friend or relative is critically ill we are apt to jump to the conclusion that the person is about to die. Certainly that is a possibility. But a crisis in the realm of medicine refers to another possibility as well, for it means a turning point in the particular illness. While the patient may indeed, at that point, "take a turn for the worse," he or she may also "take a turn for the better." The decisive thing (and our English word *crisis* comes from the Greek verb that means "to decide" — *krino*) is whether, at the critical moment, the patient is given the right kind of care.

This, it seems to me, is how we ought to regard our Canadian crisis. If Canada doesn't die, it may get better! If it doesn't succumb to the many-sided malaise from which it is suffering, our young country may, at this most critical juncture of its life, begin to grow up. We have had a hard time maturing. From the beginning we have been in a state of uncertain health as a nation: always unsure of ourselves, always waiting to be directed, always craving recognition, always depending upon outside interests to keep us in business. Always . . . becoming. Now, like a promising but diffident youth, we have come to the greatest crisis. The turning point.

And we may die! That is a serious possibility with which every Canadian must reckon. Crisis means: Canada could come to an end. Whether the end is a "bang" or a "whimper," to use T.S. Eliot's famous contrast, is not the basic issue. Whether the Canadian experiment is terminated overnight by some new phase of the world crisis, or just gradually fades away on account of economic factors stronger than our will to survive — whether, in other words, it is a quick death or a lingering one is no doubt an important consideration. But in either case it is national death we are contemplating. In fact, there are some among us who believe that the death in question has already happened, in principle at least. At the end of his moving and melancholy autobiography, *Canada Made Me,* the expatriot Canadian novelist, Norman Levine, writes:

> I wondered why I felt so bitter about Canada. After all, it was part of a dream, an experiment that could not come off. It was foolish to believe that you can take the throwouts, the rejects, the human kickabouts from Europe and tell them: Here you have a second chance. Here you can start a new life. But no one ever mentioned the price one had to pay; how much of oneself you had to betray.[3]

Other analysts of Canada's demise point to our lack of binding traditions, the artificiality of the federal system, the fact that we are a "branch-plant culture."

It is foolish to dismiss these more drastic analyses of the Canadian condition. But in choosing the language of crisis I am implying that, while the "end" is a real prospect, it is neither an accomplished fact nor an inevitability. Canada may die; but on the other hand it may gain strength, find itself, and pass from the state of an adolescent "becoming" to something a little more mature — just at this turning point!

As in all crises, what will make the difference is the right kind of care.

Who Cares?

Surely that is the heart of the matter. In great measure, the most serious aspect of the Canada crisis is the lack of passionate and informed caring for "this vexing and marvellous country."[4] Who really cares about Canada? Who, among those who do care, are both passionate and informed in their caring?

The writers of the Task Force report[5] and many others assure us that "a great many Canadians" display "an intense love of their country and a deep concern for its future." Passion, then, may not be altogether missing. But genuine passion involves a search for understanding. Without being informed, passion is too often just a by-product of sentiment. Obviously there is a good deal of sentiment abroad these days. Many people vow they won't let Canada die, and some of the more passionate profess they will even go to war to keep our country together — which seems strange logic. But care is more than sentiment. Sentiment, however passionate, never kept anyone or anything from dying, least of all institutions like nations. Care includes understanding, trying to get to the bottom of the malaise, facing the real problems and not settling for arguments about the symptoms. Care involves thinking, not just opinionating. It means working, not only weeping. It entails watchfulness and self-criticism and sacrifice. Above all, care clings fast to the prospect that life and not death can be the outcome of the crisis. Unlike sentiment, which for all its fine protestations often acts as though it were all up with the poor patient, care is a consequence of hope. Hope against hope!

Such care seems hard to find today — care for Canada, I mean. It is not difficult to find individuals and groups who care for aspects, dimensions, or regions of our country, but as a Canadian historian has said, "The nation must be something greater than the sum of its parts. If it is not so, it ceases to exist, it has lost the will to continue."[6] Caring for this or that tangible or intangible quality of Canadian life — our vastness, our relative freedom and affluence, our peaceful approach — is not to be equated with caring for Canada, nor is caring for this or that region — the Maritimes, the Prairies, or Quebec. Regional pride need not be *anti*-Canadian. It will in fact be one of the basic points of this study that caring for the parts (regions) and caring for the whole (Canada) are not only compatible but belong together. Being creatures of time and space, we can only develop a feeling for the whole by beginning with some part. Each of us has his or her roots in some quite specific place or places — a village in Southwestern Ontario, a town in Nova Scotia, a farm near Swift Current, a section of Montréal. It is natural that we should have a special feeling for our own home, local culture, linguistic group. But unless this particular identity and loyalty in some way opens us to the larger "home and native land," it is likely to perform the opposite function, and may become a barrier to caring for Canada rather than a way into such caring.

Too much of what passes for patriotism in Canada today is the kind of attachment to this or that part of the country which is nurtured by suspicion of all the other parts, or some of them in particular. It is a defensive and parochial patriotism, which depends on being against something rather than for something. When it isn't against "the Americans" it's against other regions of Canada. There are reasons — serious ones — why this kind of suspicion informs our society. Some parts of Canada *are* exploited by other parts. Canada as a whole *is* threatened by American economic and cultural dominance. But even though legitimate causes for regional defensiveness may be found along with attitudes that are not so legitimate, this does not lessen the destructive effect of a narrowly defined "provincial" patriotism. When love of region devolves into regional*ism* it saps the human spirit of its capacity for caring for the whole. A pride which might have become the occasion for generating a larger human concern becomes instead a way of limiting the access of a society to the greater community. It seems to me obvious that there is no room in the world today for that kind of pride. This small, interdependent community named earth will no longer bear such pride, whether it is called tribalism, regionalism, nationalism, or whatever else.[7]

It is somehow ironic that more Canadians today than formerly seem trapped in a psychic "localism" in spite of the fact that we have been exposed to our country physically in a way undreamt of by our forebears. We have travelled from coast to coast in campers. We have met hundreds of people from other parts of the country. We have spent many hours watching television, by means of which we have amassed a good deal of information about the rest of Canada. Yet our current, "active" generations seem to have less feeling for the country as a whole than the grandparental and earlier generations who had none of these "benefits".

I remember my own grandfather telling me about the West: the enormous fields — bigger than his entire Southern Ontario farm; the courageous spirit of the people, who had to face terrible conditions of cold and drought; the sense of community and neighbourliness one found there, especially their wonderful ways of welcoming "the stranger." With tears in his eyes (because he loved animals as well as human beings) he told me about cows, shipped from the east, who had been frozen into the mud of their corrals by a sudden blizzard, and how their new owners had been reduced to despair. He loved the West.

He had never been there. His one big trip was to the Chicago World Fair. Otherwise he remained on his farm — there was no alternative. But it wasn't necessary for him to go there in order to know and love that part of his country. He knew his own farm, his own animals, his own neighbours. That particular part, being loved, was his entrée into the rest. Given a little curiosity and imagination! Given a little grace!

Perhaps that sort of magnitude is rare. I suspect it may be rarer today than it used to be, though I have no cause to champion the past. Nevertheless, such caring seems to me to be a potentiality of the human spirit — given a little grace! If it is not, then we had better shift our metaphor right away from the language of crisis to the language of lament. Unless that kind of caring can be unearthed, evoked, or somehow created, the "patient" in question will die. Mere sentiment will not keep Canada going. Regional loyalty left to itself could easily end in balkanization — a whimpering sort of end, but still an end. Our only hope — at the turning point — is the emergence of a right kind of caring *about the whole.* [8]

I am writing this book to do whatever I can to stimulate that human potentiality for the care of nation.

Why Should *Christians* Care?

Why should a Christian theologian want to elicit such care in the first place? Isn't there something incongruous about Christians looking for ways of bolstering the concern for nation? One would have thought, perhaps, that Christians ought by definition to be internationalists, since the love of God knows no boundaries.

In a real sense, everything that follows must address itself implicitly to this question. But an explicit answer at the beginning may help to clarify some basic assumptions. While this study is not written "for Christians only" — and certainly not for the kinds of Christians who no longer wrestle with human problems, passions and doubts — it does assume that there is "a Christian perspective" on "the Canada crisis." It assumes, as well, that through exposure to that perspective we might expect some increase in "passionate and informed" care for our nation. How then ought we to address the suggestion that this kind of concern and search does not really belong to Christian faith and life?

i *Not Nationalism but Care of Nation:* In the first place, we should be clear that it is not the task of Christian theology to provide a basis for Canadian nationalism as such. Nationalism is an ideology — a theory about reality which is no longer open to actual experience but determines in advance how experience shall be interpreted.[9] Christians have an innate suspicion of all ideologies; they suspect that reality is always bigger than our ideas of it.

Yet to reject an *ism* is not necessarily to reject the truth that gave rise to the *ism*. To back away in horror from the fanaticism which can turn love of nation into hatred for all the rest is not to back away from all love for one's nation. Accordingly, what I want to attempt here is a Christian rationale for the care of our nation, the kind of care that could help us as a people in a state of "protracted crisis" to take a turn for the better.

Among other things this means that I shall challenge the reader to think about Canada on the basis of a Christian frame of reference. How, from the side of their own faith and tradition, can Christian people assess the Canada crisis above their immediate "natural" identities as Anglophones, Francophones, New Canadians, Original Canadians, and the like, and grasp that "little bit of grace" that brings imagination and hope to life? How can they bring to bear on our national crisis a perspective that does not simply cloak party, racial, ethnic, political and other "isms" but is rooted in a genuine stewardship of the world and its creatures? So much of what Christian individuals and bodies *are* saying and doing in Canada today (especially, it seems to me, in Anglophone Canada) is little more than a stained glass version of what is being said and done by their own ethnic and class counterparts in the society at large. Against that temptation, I want to ask: Can we think about Canada, and act within it, as Christians? Can we enter seriously into that struggle with all the things in our own individual and collective spirits which resist the Christian perspective and cling to ''the party line?''

ii *Not Internationalism but Vigilance for Humanity:* It is frequently assumed, implicitly if not explicitly, that true Christians must be internationalists in outlook and aim; consequently, that any special concern for ''the nation'' is a sort of betrayal of authentic Christian sentiment.

There is a basis in truth behind this assumption, though it is distorted. What the Christian is committed to is not an ideology — not even a rather admirable ideology like internationalism. The Christian is committed to humanity. Being committed to God means being committed to that which God himself is committed: ''the world'' (John 3:16).

That, of course, conditions very decisively the character of one's commitment to one's own country. As a Christian, my primary ''horizontal'' commitment is to the human community in its entirety. For all human beings, regardless of their race, sex, nation, tongue, age, size, intelligence — without exception are beloved creatures of the God in whom I try to believe. The distinction between those who command my most immediate attention and energies and those who do not is drawn, not on the basis of race, sex, nation, but only on the basis of need — *their* need. All are ''the neighbour.'' But those who ''fall amongst the thieves'' — the poor, the oppressed, the hungry and sick — have priority.

Nothing is said about the priority of ''my own.'' The scriptures frequently warn against the human tendency to give first consideration to one's own self, family, race, homeland. The rudimentary truth from which Christian ''internationalism'' has sprung lies in this recognition of the tendency of human egocentrism to nurture and preserve only what belongs to the self.

But what the internationalist, universalist Christian sentiment does not grasp — what in fact it frequently hides — is the
equally strong human temptation to slide out from underneath
concrete responsibility for *any* neighbour in the name of serving
all! The sin of pride always enters the picture in my feeling for
my own, it is true, but sin has another side as well: sloth. And
sloth forever looks for opportunities to avoid the very real neighbour who knocks at the door at midnight. Frequently sloth finds
such opportunities tucked away inside high ideals! Throughout
the history of the church there have been very idealistic Christians who under the aegis of loving the transcendent Father and
the universal brother were able to avoid all particular loves and
other inconveniences of human relationships. But there is
simply no route to the universal which does not run through the
particular. There is no way to "the world" that God "so loves"
which does not run through the dark streets of Bethlehem and
the Via Dolorosa of Jerusalem.

It is even possible that, on occasion, the particular through
which one is led to the universal is precisely "one's own." It
was that way for my grandfather, who was able to love the vast
Canadian prairies he had never seen because he deeply cared for
what he had seen. And how many of us are there who had to
become fathers and mothers ourselves before children began to
have great significance for us — the kind of significance, for
instance, that can make one alarmed about the future our
generation is preparing for tomorrow's children?

It is quite possible that Canadian Christians and others could
be exercising the most direct kind of international responsibility
available to them today by developing a responsible care for
their own nation. For in addition to the general truth that one's
own can often be the way into a larger human concern, there is
the historic reality that Canada at present could play a very
significant role for good in the world community.[10] The Third
World, for example, could come to look upon Canada as a
friendly power, without overt imperial designs, without
"messages" to bear from other empires, either! In some small
measure (but it is altogether too small in relation to the need)
something like this has occasionally occurred. But the full ex-

ploration of such a posture in the international community is prevented by the fact that we Canadians have not evolved any clear-cut role of this sort for ourselves. For the most part, we have not even shown the inclination to do so. We have not sought an identity sufficiently distinct from the other "empires" with which we are historically and geographically linked (especially the United States); hence we are not perceived by the rest of the world, on the whole, as a national community sufficiently mature to be trusted with the deepest concerns of its neighbours. In short, we are prevented from being the kind of catalytic and mediating people we could be in today's "global village" because of the Canada Crisis.

It therefore becomes the responsibility, not only of Christians but of all who are trying to be vigilant for humanity in these times, to concern themselves with our national condition. Here, national care rightly pursued is not an alternative to international concern but a way of expressing the latter concretely.

iii Not alone but in a Community of Caring: The search for a *Christian* rationale for the care of nation does not take place in isolation from others who are also searching for reasons for their hope. There can be no thought of "going it alone." Christians who behave as if going it alone were desirable, or even possible, have not yet awakened to the fact that Christendom is over: that is, that the Western world is no longer a Christian world; that the church can no longer behave as if it were the official cult of the whole society and every citizen's conscience; that we are by now a minority, a *diaspora,* one alternative in the midst of a religiously pluralistic society. This need not reduce us to despair and nostalgia and mere "survivalism." The only Christians who despair over the humiliation of Christendom are those who want to go it alone, and who cannot separate the gospel from the kind of theological triumphalism and ecclesiastical imperialism that has accompanied it for so many centuries. What the recognition of the new status of the church in the world ought on the contrary to produce is the sense that we are free at last, after centuries of pretending to go it alone as the official religion of civilization, to be present in the world as a prophetic minority ("seed," "salt," "yeast," "a candle"), recognizing God's work wherever we find it.

The community of faith does not have to go it alone because God himself is there before us, doing what must be done to keep life from devolving into totally inhuman forms. Alone, we are certainly not capable of that. Alone in Canada today, Christians are quite incapable of demonstrating the kind of care I have said can make the difference between life and death for our country in its crisis state. All that we may hope to do, if we are imaginative enough in exploring our own Christian reasons for the care of nation, is to find other persons, groups and movements whose attempts at caring may be encouraged and sometimes inspired by our own. Authentic care, including care for this nation, is a rare thing in the world today. But it is not altogether absent. Now and then it is conspicuous, mostly it is dormant, sometimes it is even hidden beneath its apparent opposite — indifference, cynicism, escape. The God who cares does not leave his world without witnesses and ambassadors of his caring. Some of them are bound to be (for many Christians) "strange bedfellows." The task of prophetic faith however is not to withhold ourselves from these unusual alliances, but to be wise enough about the character of God's caring for the earth and its peoples to be able to recognize his witnesses and ambassadors no matter under what unlikely disguises — and to make common cause with them. To become part of the Community of the Caring.

It has been said that ours is "the me generation" (Tom Wolfe). A recent perceptive study of North American culture describes us as a "narcissistic" people, a society of "diminishing expectations," where security and pleasure for the self seem the only goals worth pursuing.[11] If Canada is suffering from a lack of passionate and informed care today, and may indeed die of that lack, the malaise is not entirely unique to Canada. It is perhaps the most notorious feature of the whole Western world.

However discouraging such a phenomenon may be, there are some "happy issues" to be gleaned in the midst of these sufferings. One of them is the way in which, in just such a care-less world, those who *do* care are better able to recognize and fraternize with one another. Even if their care is based on very different, even incompatible reasons; even if they "come at" their common problems from all sorts of incommensurate points of view, they recognize the problems as common to all. That in itself is something! Beyond that, they frequently discover that different accounts of "what is" and "what ought to be" can nevertheless lead to the same or similar conclusions as to "what can be done." And on occasion it may even lead to the discovery that there are, after all, different ways of saying and thinking the same thing!

Our Agenda

Our task in what follows, then, is to try to think and articulate "our thing" about Canada — our "Christian perspective." But we shall do so in the anticipation that if we can do it with sufficient imagination and grace, others who "are not of this fold" will sometimes think: "It's the same thing." We cannot ask the others to recognize our specific words, terms, or historical reference-points. We cannot expect them to tell our same story. But we can expect that their stories, words, historic references, and metaphors will sometimes be in essence the same thing. In fact we can assume that all human stories and theories which have their genesis in an ultimate concern for humanity and the earth may in the last analysis be halting attempts expressing the same thing, namely God's concern for humanity and earth. As God's concern transcends all our expressions of it, so each of our expressions may help enrich the others. What we may hope, as Christians who try to explore the meaning of God's concern for humanity and earth within the specifics of the Canadian dimension, is that our particular ways of reflecting upon the Canada crisis will help to elicit from others who do not use our language, the greater capacity for caring that is part of their own human potential. And then there may be the kind of increase of care that is needed at this turning point, if life and not death is to ensue.

Our particular way of reflecting upon the human condition generally, and therefore also upon the Canadian condition in the moment, involves two poles or foci, each with its own terminology and its own historical reference-points. One pole (we may think of it, temporarily, as the negative pole — but "negative" and "positive" are strangely inter-related in this story) is usually named "sin." The other (positive) focus is conventionally called "redemption." In this story, for reasons I shall try to make clear at the right moment, we are going to concentrate upon a particular aspect of the Christian theology of redemption, namely hope. Correspondingly, the negative focus will centre upon one of the primary aspects of sin in the Christian tradition — *despair.*

What insights can be brought to the analysis of Canada's crisis from the vantage-point of this double-edged (dialectical) tradition of Christian anthropology? No doubt the choice of aspects of the two foci (hope and despair),[12] taken together with some of the things I have said heretofore, already suggest the line of analysis that is to follow. However, as I have just now warned, it should not be assumed that opposites or polarities in Christian theology can be set over against one another in a simple or predictable way. It does not happen in theology that way any more than it happens in physics. The surprising element is always the interaction between opposites — as for instance St Paul knew when he wrote, "when I am weak then I am strong." It is for example by no means a foregone conclusion that what is usually thought hopeful is really hope in Christian terms or, conversely, that what is usually regarded as the stuff of despair is really despair as Christian faith sees it. This religion has had from the beginning a way of "turning things upside down" (See Acts 17:6). It may be, then — to translate all this into the specific subject of our present deliberations — that the most *hopeful* thing about contemporary Canada in crisis is its beginnings of a capacity for *despair!*

However that may be, the two parts of the study are determined by these two foci — sin / despair and redemption / hope. They have to be treated separately for the sake of ordering our thought. But in the reality of our day-to-day struggle in the world at large and in Canada too, they are by no means separable.

I
"The Winter of our Discontent"

1
Canada
Come of Age?

The Argument

Twentieth-century Christian theology found it had to speak about the world in the "drastic" language of sin and redemption. Heretofore it has seemed inappropriate to apply such terms to the Canadian experience. Now it appears that the Age of Anxiety has enveloped Canada too. This is a painful experience, but it could be "the beginning of wisdom" — and (in the best sense) of Nationhood.

Strong Language!

After about a century of "liberalism" at the helm of the ship of theology and church, the twentieth century had hardly begun when Christian theologians in Europe found it necessary to return to the strong language of the Bible to speak about the human situation. Liberalism, following closely the spirit of eighteenth and nineteenth century optimism about man, emphasized the human potential ("under God," of course) for rationality, goodness, and mastery of the earth. It found that it was quite possible to adapt the *essential* message of the gospel to the Modern world. It discarded the dark language of sin. It interpreted the biblical concept of redemption in evolutionary and immanental terms. And it found in the scriptural symbol of the kingdom of God a way of expressing the general feeling of the day, that humanity is progressing gradually but surely towards the realization of an harmonious, peaceable and "perfect" society. "Every day in every way, we're getting better and better."

For the most sensitive Europeans this vision was shattered by "the guns of August." My teacher Paul Tillich, who was one of those sensitive Europeans, used always to tell us: "The nineteenth century ended on 1 August 1914." In a dramatic way, the First World War (which in my childhood was still called "The Great War") made perfectly clear to such persons what other, less noisy events had already caused them to suspect: the "liberal" view of the human condition was simply incapable of taking in the negative side of historical existence.

What the Great War and its underlying spiritual malaise did for Christian theology was to send its best architects "back to the drawing board" — literally, back to the original sources: the scriptures, the Fathers, the Reformers. Since the theological conventions they had inherited were incapable of acknowledging radical evil, let alone confronting it, the theologians had to ask themselves: Is Christianity as a whole bankrupt in the face of the Modern world and its shattering, or is there something in this faith that our own mentors and forebears neglected — or discarded? The more persistent amongst these investigators found that something had indeed been omitted. Perhaps it was the essence of the gospel!

That, at any rate, is what was suggested by the first really powerful analysis coming out of these new theological investigations. This was Karl Barth's *Romans*[13]; it "fell like a bomb into the playyard of the theologians" (Karl Holl). In it, Barth discusses the life of humanity in terms quite abhorrent to liberal optimism and progressivism. The world, he says, can only be understood in terms of sin — not mere ignorance, immorality, or underachievement, but a fundamental abrogation of life's foundational relationships: the relation to God, to our fellow human beings, to our total environment. Nor is redemption built into the historical process. It is a matter of sheer grace — an "impossible possibility." Thus hope, which liberalism had equated with the official optimism of the modern world, was for Barth an attitude of pure trust in the light of all the evidence to the contrary.

This is Abraham's faith: faith which, *in hope against hope*, steps out beyond human capacity across the chasm which separates God and man, beyond the visibility of the seen and the invisibility of the unseen world, beyond subjective and objective possibility.[14]

It is not accidental (and from the perspective of this present study not incidental either) that the first nomenclature applied to this new theology was "the Theology of Crisis."

Barth's reading of the world and of the gospel did not lend itself easily to Modern society, even in its shattered condition. Where that shattering could still be kept to a minimum, or hidden beneath apparent success, the resistance of Christians against such a drastic analysis of existence continued to be very strong — in particular in the English-speaking world. Only gradually has a Theology of Crisis (under various names and slogans) made its hesitant way into the Anglo-Saxon part of the Modern world. The explanation for this is not a great mystery. For a variety of reasons, mostly economic, the Anglo-Saxon world has been able to fend off the "shattering" of the Modern world view for a longer time than most other parts of the globe. We have been affluent; we have been powerful; we have been victors in two "Great Wars." It could *seem* to us, for a considerably longer period, that man is still rational and good, that his mastery of nature is inevitable and desirable, that history is progressing visibly, just as every new model of the automobile could seem better than the last. In other words, the liberal vision of the world could seem to us still a viable one. We did not experience life as crisis; therefore we did not need a theology of crisis.

In time, however, perceptive minds in the theological communities of the Anglo-Saxon world also began to reflect on the world in something like Barth's terms. In Britain no less a figure than Archbishop William Temple wrote in 1938, almost wistfully:

If we began our work again today, its perspectives would be different.... I am conscious of a certain transition of interest in our minds, as in the minds of theologians all over the world.... If the security of the nineteenth century, already shattered in Europe, finally crumbles away in our country too, we shall be pressed more and more towards a theology of Redemption.... A theology of Redemption.... tends.... to sound the prophetic note; it is more ready to admit that much in this evil world is irrational and strictly unintelligible.... (If such becomes our emphasis) we shall be coming closer to the New Testament. We have been learning again how impotent man is to save himself, how deep and pervasive is that corruption which theologians call Original Sin. Man needs above all else to be saved from himself. This must be the work of Divine Grace.[15]

Even in the United States (which was entering a new phase of prosperity when Temple spoke these words), a few Christians were already turning away from liberalism towards the strong language of sin and redemption. In 1938 one of the most articulate of the theologies of redemption for which Temple was tentatively calling, was being prepared by Reinhold Neibuhr in the form of his Gifford Lectures for the fateful year of 1939.[16] Liberal theology in America at that time could not fathom why a Christian professor in the midst of the most progressive society on earth would want to discuss the human condition in such pessimistic terms as Niebuhr did in his books, sermons, and lectures. But by the mid 1960s, when Neibuhr died, the position he had taken seemed closer to the truth. By that time the United States had been involved in a variety of social and economic experiences (including less than honourable, less than successful wars) which had brought society close to a state of conspicuous crisis and "future shock." By that time, too, many other voices in the world of Christian faith had joined the Barths, Niebuhrs, Temples, and others who had re-thought the faith in the strong language of sin and redemption.

These men and women have been our teachers and mentors — all of us who have studied theology; all of us who have heard or preached sermons, or participated in study groups. These interpreters have helped us to reflect on the world from the perspective of biblical and doctrinal categories very different from the ones bequeathed to us by the Modern world. They have prepared us to consider a future for the human race which, far from being "surprise free," probably holds even greater crises than we have so far had to endure or contemplate — to consider such a future, yet to explore the hope that is in us.[17]

So far we seem to have been able to do all this without applying it specifically to our own society — to Canada!

Canada, the Exception

Perhaps it was just that we felt no call to do so. We could use the strong language about mankind in general. We could read about the disintegration of Western civilization and the future shock experienced by the Americans, but Canada has seemed perfectly intact; its future has appeared secure. Somehow Canada has seemed, until now, the exception. It has kept the shattering of the Modern vision at a distance.

Of course, part of the reason for the failure of the Canadian theological community to apply the strong language of critical theology to the Canadian situation, is the result of a certain tendency within that community itself. It is not that we have lacked awareness of these theological currents, but rather that we have lacked the courage and the habit of indigenous application and expression. Like most other things Canadian, Canadian theology is most suspect by us when it is consciously Canadian. Canadians do not trust their own. Canadian theologians do not trust their own intuition.

This propensity of the Canadian mentality as a whole is doubly effective when it comes to Christian theology. For in all of our ecclesiastical communities, the mother Church (whether in terms of administration or origins) is located in Europe (Rome, Canterbury, Geneva, Edinburgh). Moreover, our general "colonial" status has prevented us from trusting our own imagination and experience sufficiently to produce even the degree of originality put forward by American Christians — though they share our deference to Europe. Our theological communities have always been heavily laced with non-Canadian teachers, and thus Canadian ministers and laity have been indoctrinated in British, European, and American theological traditions with very little attempt to relate all this to the specifics of the Canadian situation.

The upshot is that theology in anglophone Canada is perhaps the least contextual of all Christian theology in the contemporary world. We are able to laud the development of "indigenous" theological postures in Africa, Asia and South America, but we ourselves labour under some kind of almost constitutional hesitancy. Instead of trying, through deeper participation in our own context and its struggles, to find an appropriate analysis and response from the Christian tradition, we repeat nearly verbatim the ideas which come out of other people's political, cultural, and theological struggles.

If the overall analysis in this study is correct, then the rudimentary reason for our hesitancy as a theological community is that heretofore the Canadian experience has been sufficiently "crisis free" to afford all our intellectuals — including theologians — the luxury of pursuing ideas without having to test their adequacy in relation to real life. If it is true that our society has now entered the critical state affecting all Western peoples, it may be that our intellectuals will increasingly be denied this luxury and themselves, as persons and thinkers, be thrust into the fray. Nothing could be better for the state of academe — including Christian theology. We shall either become contextual at this turning point, or we shall fade out with all the others who do not have the wherewithal or the courage to enter the dark place that is the future of Canada, humanity and earth.

It is true, however, that until this point in our history, overtly Canadian conditions have not lent themselves to the kind of spiritual and intellectual struggling and suffering that is almost a precondition for depth of thought. While students of theology over the past fifty years in Canada have learned how to reflect upon human existence along the lines of the great European and American theologians of our century, the kind of world assumed by the Bonhoeffers, Bultmanns, and Barths has not been our Canadian world — at least on the surface. We could empathize to some extent with Barth facing the Nazis or Bonhoeffer in his prison or Niebuhr locked in mortal conflict with American big business. But our own immediate world, Canada, seemed less "black and white." We did not necessarily exempt Canada from the predicamental character of the world which became the general theme of Christian and other deliberations especially after World War II, but neither were we moved to give our country a specific place within such a discussion. Helmut Thielicke in defeated Germany could write a devastating book about the modern world under the title, *Nihilism.* But nihilism in Canada? Hardly likely!

In our quiet way, we were rather of the opinion that by some happy accident (perhaps even by divine providence) Canada had been spared. Spared not only the great physical catastrophies of our European, South American, and even American neighbours, but spared also the failure of nerve, the self-doubt, or the outright despair that accompanied and may have precipitated these ''foreign'' catastrophies. Our tendency was to regard our nation as young and rather innocent. (I remember how shocked I was when, in the early 1950s, I heard Reinhold Niebuhr say that ''the Canadians are not less vulgar than we are, but only less powerful.'') We did not remove Canada altogether from the world crisis to which our theology and our newspapers continued to point, yet we felt that Canada was somehow different. It was a kind of potentiality, a reality not yet achieved, but in the building and, on the whole, going in the right direction. Our collective sentiments could be expressed in the words of the Canadian historian George W. Brown, who concluded his *Building the Canadian Nation* with this assessment of Canada in the post-World War II years:

> Canada thus found herself in a world torn by conflict. Almost every year brought its crisis, and over all loomed the threat of the atomic and hydrogen bombs which were capable of destroying mankind itself. Perhaps, indeed, it was this terrible new threat which held the nations back from a third world war. And yet it was a world of hope as well as conflict and fear. Never had there been such exciting possibilities of advancement through science, or so much effort of nations to help one another through international organizations. In this world Canada felt her new responsibilities as a nation. Lying as she did in a strategic place on the world map, and with her close friendships with Britain and the Commonwealth,

France and the United States, she had a place of influence much greater than she could have foreseen. To use this influence wisely yet imaginatively was in mid-twentieth century Canada's greatest *challenge.* [18]

It would be wrong to mistake this modest statement of Canada's place in the contemporary world for blatant national messianism. That was (and is) not our Canadian style. Not that we are too modest for it, we are just too small. Nor does Brown's assessment exempt Canada from the world predicament. How could it? "The bomb" of which he speaks would not "exempt" Canada! Nonetheless, his statement assigns our homeland a special rôle in the future of mankind; and it assumes, implicitly, a kind of innocency, inner strength, self-awareness, and above all a cohesiveness and unity without which such a rôle could not even be envisaged. Moreover, it phrases all of this in the language of "challenge" — not of crisis. Not in Canada!

If therefore Christian theology has not manifested a capacity for applying the theology of sin and redemption in the Canadian context, it is not only because of our failure as a community of faith to think our theology indigenously. It is also because the condition necessary for imaginative contextual thought — the condition of crisis — has been late in coming to us.

But Now . . .

The revised edition of Professor Brown's study of Canada was published in 1958. Only a few, I suspect, of those who read it would have pondered the fact that a major study of Canada by a Canadian professor of history was publishd by "JM Dent & Sons *(Canada) Limited.*" A scant seven years later, another book appeared, and for significant numbers of anglophone Canadians it achieved — along with the events to which it pointed — the kind of consciousness which made us begin to take notice of such little symbols of our actual national status as "brackets Canada Limited." This book was called *Lament For A Nation.* [19] Its sub-title was still more arresting: "The Defeat of Canadian Nationalism."

The lament was written by one of Canada's foremost scholars, the political philosopher George Grant. It was immediately occasioned by the Defense Crisis of 1962–63. That crisis, Grant believed, marked the point at which the Canadian government and people made it openly clear that they were in no way prepared to steer a course in any kind of independence from the USA. Grant saw the defeat of John Diefenbaker, who had opposed the American-backed insistence that Canada should arm the Bomarc missles with atomic warheads, as a token of the de facto demise of Canada. Diefenbaker's "inability to govern (he wrote) is linked with the inability of this country to be sovereign."[20] And in a line of argument hitherto largely unsung by our intellectuals, he argued that "for twenty years before its defeat in 1957, the Liberal party had been pursuing policies that led inexorably to the disappearance of Canada."[21] He understood his analysis of Canada's demise as (almost) an argument after the fact. It had to be in the form of a lament therefore, like the *Lamentations* attributed to Jeremiah. His book, as he puts it . . .

> . . . makes no practical proposals for our survival as a nation. It argues that Canada's disappearance was a matter of necessity. But how can one lament necessity — or, if you will, fate? The noblest of men love it; the ordinary accept it; the narcissists rail against it. But I lament it as a celebration of memory; in this case, the memory of that tenuous hope that was the principle of my ancestors. The insignificance of that hope in the endless ebb and flow of nature does not prevent us from mourning. At least we can say with Richard Hooker: "Posterity may know that we have not loosely through silence permitted things to pass away as in a dream.[22]

In Brown's statement, in keeping with the mood of challenge still prevalent in the 1950s, hope is future-oriented. In Grant's book, with the capitulation of Canada to the "universal and homogeneous state" whose "imperial centre" is the USA, hope has become "hope remembered."

Naturally Grant's analysis was and still is regarded by many as a gross exaggeration of our national condition. Such an analysis is hardly the sort of thing to be promoted by the Chamber of

Commerce! Yet Grant's is by no means a single voice in the wilderness. A whole generation of younger Canadian thinkers has by now felt itself exposed to the raw data of what Professor Grant laments. Many besides Grant have noted how disinterested anglophone Canadians seem to be in their own story, their past, their future as a people. Many have expatiated on the theme broached in the introduction to this study — the scarcity of those who care for the country as a whole. *Canada: Cancelled Because of Lack of Interest*, announces one supposedly humourous title.[23] More serious studies fill in the concrete details of this national capitulation — its consequences at the level of economics, foreign relations, education,[24] communications, art and literature, tourism. One generalization about the state of our country is put forward by a leading literary figure, Margaret Atwood. She insists that the great theme uniting all or most Canadian imaginative literature is not hope, or "becoming," or innocence, or the beauty and grandeur of nature, or any of the other themes our earlier indoctrination taught us to anticipate but . . . *survival*. Sheer survival![25] Hardly the sort of thing one would have expected from the land of *Anne of Green Gables!* But the thesis must be taken very seriously, for art is perhaps the most telling indication of a people's real state. As Marshall McLuhan has said, "I think of art, at its most significant, as a DEW line, a Distant Early Warning system that can always be relied on to tell the old culture what is beginning to happen to it."[26]

The events in French Canada, culminating with the 15 November 1976 election of the Parti Québecois and pointing toward referenda which may end by dividing the country permanently, only makes more graphic the bewilderment present for all reflective Canadians. To have moved from the vision of Canada still implied in Brown's 1958 "challenge" to the survivalist realities of our present, is to have been translated almost overnight from one world into another. It is to have experienced what so many other peoples in the Modern Western world have experienced before us: the end of the Modern vision, the bankruptcy of both cultural and theological liberalism for interpreting and coping with our actual experience. This "end of an era" now becomes the lot of a people which only yesterday seemed to have been passed over by the angel of death, who throughout this century has been turning the fondest dreams of post-Renaissance man to dust and ashes. To be sure, our version of this dreaming was a little different; thus our experience of its termination also has important differences. Canadian liberalism, the special champion of our New World optimism, saw "paradise (as) a low-key variant of the American dream." Canadian liberalism did not "have the heady totality of American liberalism;" moreover, it "had to face significant challenges on both the right and the left."[27] It is possible that these differences could play a significant part in our attempt to find a basis for new forms of hope.[28]

But we have first to face the crisis that is upon us. If we want to speak about hope in a genuine and not just a sentimental way, we must confront the reality of our despair. If we intend to apply the category of redemption in some credible sense to our Canadian situation, we have first to contemplate that situation in the perspective of the other, negative focus of the Christian story: sin. Events have by now provided the condition necessary for the application of this strong language. Canada has come of age — not in the progressive sense of the term, but in the critical sense: it has entered the Modern World, the world in crisis. Late in time our land has joined its Western contemporaries in the Age of Anxiety.

On Getting Used to the Dark

Upon entering a dark and uncertain place, one's first reaction is to flee. The sense of wanting to run, to "escape," belongs to contemporary experience. The temptation to escape from the realities of our Canadian situation today is a species of the universal flight from history that characterizes our century. It expresses itself on the one hand in attempts to return to nature,[29] in the pursuit of otherworldly religions (some of them "Christian"), and in less lofty pursuits connected with drugs, sex, violence. On the other hand it expresses itself in the loss of certain former values: our lack of feeling for community, our pervasive cynicism about government, our distrust of most institutions, the flighty character of human relationships including marriage and family.

It is understandable and human to want to escape, for historical existence has become very difficult — critical! Old certitudes have vanished. There is little one can really depend upon — as a parent, for example, who can rely upon any support from the community at large? One feels alone, alienated in one's own land. Homes and families have lost the dimension of security. Governments do not govern. Educators do not educate. Industries and institutions, burdened with strikes and the rising costs of production, do not produce. Workers, feeling no sense of purpose in their work, are reduced to drones. Canada itself, which used to seem so stable (even if it never really was), has become "hope remembered," — but hardly even remembered by the majority. It is natural to want to flee from the consciousness of the dark place that our history has become.

But there is a more courageous way of reacting to the dark place. It is to find, somehow, the will to stay there; to wait in the dark, as it were, until one's eyes are a little accustomed to it; to feel one's way about, take a few steps. Perhaps one will stumble and fall. On the other hand, after some initial awkwardness, it may grow less frightening. There may even be some light to be discerned — there, in the dark! Christians ought not to be surprised if such were the case, since they hold the faith of a light which shines in the darkness and may be seen *only* from within that darkness.

That same faith, in its earlier, Judaic form, is expressed by the great contemporary writer, Elie Wiesel, a survivor of the darkness called "Auschwitz."

> I know: the paths of the soul, overgrown, often know only the night, a very vast, very barren night, without landscapes. And yet I tell you: . . . The most glorious works of man are born in that night.[30]

Canada has seemed to us a land of light in a darkening world. Now our light too is fading. That is sad, even traumatic. But one need not despise the light that we have had in the past, as a people, to suppose that there could be a still better light. So far, our light has been the light of those who are beginning their day: the light of youth and vigour, the light of the Age of Progress — of the "Enlightenment"! That light need not be altogether despised just because it has become inadequate. But there is a still more welcome light — it is the light which sometimes is given to those "who sit in darkness and the shadow of death." Their plans have not worked out. They have not reached the promised haven. To these, if light is given (even if it is only a very small light), it can be received as no blazing sun was ever received by the human spirit.

The philosopher Hegel put it another way: "The owl of Minerva [goddess of wisdom] takes its flight at evening." In other words, only in the state of uncertainty, darkening, crisis, can people expect to find real wisdom. Until now, we Canadians have not been a very wise people. At our best we may have been bright, but we have not been wise. There has been about us a kind of innocency which, for its better part, has meant vigour and optimism, but for its worse has meant naivety, bravado, and rashness. We have neither been perceived by the rest of the world as a wise people, nor have we perceived ourselves that way. Secretly we have known ourselves to be an unsophisticated and often adolescent people. That is part of the reason why we do not trust ourselves — as business men and women, as professionals, as intellectuals, as leaders of unions or the military. We do not invest in our country financially, and we receive our own athletes and entertainers only when they have been successful in the United States or Europe. We do not feel ourselves to be a mature people, capable of judging truth and talent, capable of independence from larger empires, capable of taking our own pulse!

If "evening" is the condition necessary for mature wisdom, it could be that the evening Canada has entered is a blessing in disguise. If we do not try to escape from it, we could be the beginning of the kind of maturity we lack. We might grow up! If "the best works of man are born in the night," it could be that this strange and somehow arbitrary collection of races, linguistic groups, and "regions" *might*, under the conditions of a common crisis, become a people — a nation, in the best sense! Nations do not simply happen because of orders in council or meetings in Charlottetown. Nor are they destroyed by other meetings in Quebec City or Edmonton or the boardrooms of "branch plants" in Toronto. Nations, too, in the best sense, are products of the night — products of some light that was experienced, after darkness, by people who before the darkness had very little in common.

Israel of old — and in its way Israel today, too — is for Christians the primary example of what this means. Before the oppression of Egypt and the terrors of the wilderness, Israel was not a people but only a collection of wandering tribes. It became a people because it was subjected to crisis — to the impossibility of a future (the Red Sea), to the limits of its natural inclinations (the Babylonian captivity). Not through success, but through precisely the failure of its bright dreams, Israel found wisdom. Just as through the experience of dividedness and internal strife it discovered its true identity. Not automatically, but because there were those who cared.

Canada in crisis could become a people — a nation — in a way that a hundred years and more of "official unity" could never constitute us. But there is nothing automatic about it. Wisdom does not *always* come at "evening," nor are the best works of the human spirit *necessarily* born in every night. There is a condition. I have already said that the basic condition is caring — that enough of us should care. But caring means being prepared to stay in the dark place long enough, to wait patiently enough for real "light," to ensure that what may come to us will approximate wisdom. One thing is certain: neither wisdom nor good nor light nor anything besides chaos and confusion can occur if our only reaction to the dark is to hide from it.

2
Sin and Hope – and Their Strange Connection

The Argument

Sin can be defined by juxtaposing it with each of St Paul's three "virtues":[31] *by contrast with* **faith**, *it is* **distrust***; by contrast with* **love**, *it is* **alienation***; by contrast with* **hope** *it is* **despair***. All three meanings are always present in the reality to which the term* **sin** *points. But different situations, including different historical periods, bring one or another meaning into prominence. Our own historical period has been confronted in particular with sin as despair.*

The Connection

Entering the dark place — confronting the "negative" in the Christian analysis of human existence — always means running into the poor, beleaguered word *sin*, probably the most misunderstood word in the Christian vocabulary. Anyone who wants to use this word without being mocked by secular thought on the one hand or praised by the wrong kind of religious thought on the other, has consciously and purposely to attempt to redeem it for his use. I am proposing the application of this ancient, "drastic" word to the current Canadian situation. But before I can make that application, I must explain what the term *sin* means and how it could be used in such a context as ours to illuminate that situation and not just to make predictable religious pronouncements. In the process of interpreting the term, I hope to take the reader a certain way into its application to our particular context.

It will be useful in this process to keep the two words, *sin* and *hope*, together. The most important thing about them is their contrast — and their connection. In isolation from one another, both words pose certain difficulties of communication, and they always have. This is because each of them has again and again become confused with concepts and values in the successive cultures with which Christianity has co-habited.

In our own "modern" period — and especially in this "new world" which is, as I have said, the special offspring of the Modern epoch — *hope* has continuously been mistaken for optimism — our national philosophy of life! This spurious association has all but ruined the precious, biblical concept of hope as understood in this society by Christians; for North Americans can only hear "hope" on the lips of Christians as though it were a straightforward religious confirmation of their own officially optimistic outlook. The Optimists' Club speaks about optimism, the Christians about hope; it's really "the same thing!"

But it isn't the same thing. In reality, hope in the biblical context can only be used by and for those who know themselves to be existing in near proximity to hope's antithesis — despair. To those who sit in darkness and in the shadow of death, the precious word of hope may be spoken to introduce the "impossible possibility." At the edge of the Red Sea, where it is possible to go neither forward nor backward, a way of hope may be given. Hope in the biblical context is always . . . "costly hope." What Bonhoeffer[32] said about grace — that it must never be turned into "cheap grace," something given by God easily and received by us without pain — this must also be said of that part of grace which is hope. It must never be turned into the kind of "cheap hope" of a trivial and sentimental optimism. Such an optimism works, in any case, only when it is still possible for those who manifest it to repress the data of despair. It is hard for the poor and oppressed to be optimists. It is mostly a rich man's alternative. But hope is available to the poor — the "poor in spirit," the plain poor! In a way, you have to become poor to be a candidate for hope. Poor in spirit, poor in possibilities of your own, poor in the human capacity for rejoicing — probably also, in the last analysis, just plain poor! It is very hard for the affluent peoples of the world today to hope, because we are so conditioned to believing that all the things other people have to hope for belong to us by rights!

Juxtaposing hope with sin helps to preserve the costliness of hope. It comes to those who don't deserve it, who can't earn it, and who hardly know what to do with it — sinners. But the reverse is also true: hope helps, *via negativa*, to define what sin means. If hope has been hopelessly confused with easy optimism and consequently ruined for ordinary use, sin has suffered an even worse fate. It has constantly been mistaken for some of its consequences — for sin*s* (in the plural)! Sin has come to mean whatever a given society feared or considered wrong. Christianity has by now cohabited with a great number of worldly societies and empires. Each has had a somewhat different concept of right and wrong — sometimes vastly different, in fact. But in every case, the biblical word sin (and more often, sin*s*) has been used for whatever the society in question regarded as evil or immoral. For example, Victorian and the subsequent bourgeois societies of the European and North American continents had particular difficulty with all things sexual. Immorality in these societies would be heard by most people as implying sexual immorality. If one wanted to suggest something else (like the immoral use of money, or political immorality, or the immoral exploitation of class by class), one had to specify, because immorality had come to be a synonym for personal deviousness, more particularly for any kind of deviation from accepted sexual norms. In many minds still there is an indelible connection between sin and sex. Many lives have been ruined by this nefarious connection, but on the other hand some are still titillated by it and others make money on it. "My Sin" is the name of a perfume — surely the ultimate in understatement!

We can begin to acquire a critical perspective on this misuse of the term sin if we contrast it with hope. But this reality of human experience to which the strange little word "sin" points is a many-sided thing. Therefore, in order not to avoid other important dimensions of this reality, we should contrast it not only with hope but with other positive categories of the Hebraic-Christian tradition. It may seem arbitrary — but in the end I think it is not — if we juxtapose sin with the three attitudes or qualities of life which St Paul names in his famous "hymn to love" in First Corinthians:

> Now abideth faith, hope, love; but the greatest of these is love.

Sin is Unlove

It was the same sort of identification of sin with immorality to which I have referred, an identification prevalent in nineteenth-century Danish society, that induced Soren Kierkegaard to make his beautiful pronouncement about the meaning of sin: "The opposite of Sin is not Virtue but Love." In the context of an oppressively moralistic — an avowedly Christian moralistic society — it was necessary to redefine sin sharply in terms of *unlove*. Sin is not immorality; it is unlove.

This is surely true in a permanent way. One cannot read of Jesus' encounters with people of every condition, the obviously immoral and the supposedly moral, without coming to the (perhaps shocking) conclusion that he preferred the immoral every time. Not that he condoned immorality, or actually counselled it (as Luther was falsely accused of doing when he challenged the compulsive Philip Melanchthon to "sin boldly . . ."). But Jesus found the "moral ones" obviously untrustworthy and basically lacking in self-knowledge. Part of his energies as a teacher had to be devoted to convincing the "moral" that they *were* sinners. "Let him who is without sin amongst you cast the first stone." The great temptation of the "moral" ones was to be incapable of love. It is hardly ever possible to love in a strictly moral way. If your aim is to be quite moral, then you had probably better not try Christianity, because "the greatest" thing, for the Christian, is "love." Under the conditions of historical existence — existence in a "fallen" world — love is always a very messy business. It invariably becomes mixed up with issues of justice and fairness, with the speaking of truth, with denouncing what proceeds from greed and pride and self-preservation, and with sex too, of course — for we are none of us "pure spirits" and our love is always being enacted in physical ways that are often ambiguous, to say the least. To love is therefore always to court what the moral people regard as immorality. You cannot love and stay moderate, temperate and "in charge" — all those virtues of classical Rome and much more recent societies. The lovers — the "carers" to use a weaker synonym — have usually been unpopular with the really moral people of society. Jesus was killed by them.

That was not accidental, for at bottom sin is hate; and what calls itself morality is very often born of this same hate: hatred for life, for the flesh, for freedom and spontaneity, for innocence; hatred which expresses itself in rigidity with respect to the self and intolerance in relation to others; hatred which comes out as aloofness, or self-righteousness. Perhaps its most modern dress is indifference. To say that sin is unlove is to say that it is a form — a distorted form — of *self*-love, grounded in the rejection of life, which can accept existence only so long as it is able to achieve its own advancement, autonomy, ascendency, safety, salvation. Love is "being-with." Sin, its opposite, is the ancient human attempt at "being-alone," like God — and when human beings try it, they always end by "being-against."

"The greatest of these is love" — and therefore the greatest, most damning dimension of sin is unlove. This is always true, in each individual life, in each society. But some individual lives and some societies suffer in a particular way from the negation of love. To speak only of the latter — because in this study we are reflecting mainly upon society — there have been historical cultures which in a special sense manifested an incapacity for love. All human societies manifest this incapacity, of course; but in some periods and places it has been a rudimentary social fact. In Prussian society in the nineteenth and early twentieth centuries, for example, duty, honesty, moral uprightness in one's private life; obedience on the part of children, servants, and women; military sternness on the part of the male; and many other "virtues" of this kind constituted, not just private but also *public* oppression. It was therefore necessary for Christians of the liberal theological tradition (from Schleier-macher on) to accentuate kindness, gentleness, equality, patience, the responsibility of the stronger for the weaker, and many other characteristics associated with love. If in the process, love became somewhat sentimentalized by the liberals, their basic reason for this accentuation was the right one. In an age dominated by "morality," it was the sin of unlove which had to be attacked and changed, not for private reasons only, but for the sake of the social fabric itself.

But there are nuances in the biblical concept of sin which are still not fully captured in the juxtaposition of sin and love, profoundly and permanently true as this is. There are, moreover, historical moments — and contexts — in which another dimension of the meaning of sin, besides unlove, is called for. So we may turn to the second Pauline "virtue" — faith.

Sin is Distrust

Faith, like love, is also a condition to which, over against the way of sin, humanity "in Christ" is called. Faith thus becomes a polar term by which sin ought to be defined. Placed alongside faith as its opposite, sin must be understood as distrust. For faith means trust — trusting *in (Credo in unum Deum . . .).*

Sin is the failure to trust God, but not only "God," of course, because there is never only God; there are also neighbours; there is the whole life-support system (as our technical language today condescendingly puts it) — other animals, plants, the earth itself. Trust means trusting all of these, God and his "system," his complex ecological "network." Sin is that in us which distrusts not only God, as if in some solitary and isolated religious sense, but the whole life process. Sin is the anxiety of living out of the condition of this manifold distrust. In their separation from the source and ground of their being, Adam and Eve are no longer able to live "in the moment," in trust that they will be cared for. Their life becomes a fretful and toilful search for self-made security.

But distrust is not only an individual phenomenon. It can

characterize an entire society — indeed, a civilization! The attempt described so poignantly in Genesis 11, where a primitive society tries to secure itself against disintegration and decay by building a fortress-city with a tower (the first high-rise!), is the story of the Fall of Man applied societally. Not only in its material search, but especially in its spiritual search human society is marked by insecurity and distrust. Most of the religion in which anxious humanity indulges itself — including many popular forms of "Christianity" today — is marked by distrust and the need to find permanent security. That is what led the young Karl Barth in the *Commentary on Romans* to say that the message of the Bible is that God hates religion.[33] For religion, this questing upward to get hold of the seat of power, is the antithesis of faith. Faith means risking the future — trusting God, neighbour, biosphere. It is what Jesus was getting at when he said (perhaps the most offensive statement in the New Testament, for all we have done to make it sweet and innocuous): "Do not be anxious about tomorrow . . . Consider the lilies, consider the birds, consider the beasts . . ." (Matthew 6). How offensive to our rationality and freedom to be compared to these "lower creatures!" How offensive to our Protestant work ethic to be told to stop scurrying about!

As with love, it is permanently true to say of faith that it defines, by way of negation, what sin means. Moreover, there are historical moments when sin has had to be defined quite explicitly along the lines of distrust, and when the gospel, accordingly, had to be announced in terms of the possibility of trust — of faith! The late Middle Ages were such a time. The vision which had inspired the long Medieval period, with its union of belief and rationality, had been shattered. The institutions which had been born out of that vision (the feudal system, the Holy Roman Empire, the church with its elaborate hierarchy of authority and administration) had been left as empty shells of a former glory. Like empty shells and empty houses and minds, these institutions were full of a high potential for the demonic. Spiritual as well as physical conditions contributed to an atmosphere of debilitating insecurity everywhere — an insecurity so pervasive that even sophisticated people were anxious to spend much money and time securing "indulgences" against future chaos and punishment.

It is not surprising, then, that in this atmosphere of crippling distrust, the gospel as the sixteenth-century Protestant Reformers came to express it, had to be cast in the form of a proclamation of the gracious possibility of *trust*: "By faith are you made righteous and secure, through grace, not by works lest any man should boast" (Cf. Ephesians 2:8). "Trust" *(Vertrauen)* was Luther's primary term for "faith." If his and the other Reformers' gospel of "grace and faith alone" *(sola gratia, sola fide)* caught on, it was not entirely because they were persuasive advocates of this gospel, but rather because this was the right time for such an expression of the gospel. A society caught in the grip of manifold distrust could hear and grasp after a gracious word about the possibility of trust. When sin has become not only unlove but also individual and corporate mistrust, redemption must be announced in terms of the possibility of trust, not only the possibility of love.

Sin is Despair

But sin is also in need of the third "antithesis" — hope. Without this dimension, much in our private lives which separates us from one another and leads us into sickness of every sort would not be present in the Christian account of the human condition. Without this dimension, too, whole periods of human history and whole societies — especially our own — would find little in the Christian account of reality to illuminate them, to bring them some measure of self-knowledge.

Certainly unlove has not been wanting in our epoch! Not only in abiding forms of Victorian or bourgeois moralism, but in more subtle and devastating contemporary forms, ours has been a period of sensational unlove. Hatred would be a far more accurate term here. Divesting themselves of even the shreds of morality, whole segments of our world, whole races and nations, have engaged in slaughtering, exterminating, or economically destroying one another. Human life has become very cheap. There is, moreover, a kind of almost open nihilism surrounding the more recent wars in this century of wars. The soldiers and generals of the first and second World Wars would have been shocked by it. A film like *Apocalypse Now* depicts this nihilism graphically and horribly. It is as if life had become so unbearable, so meaningless, that it should be destroyed as systematically, as dispassionately as possible: "without judgment," as Kurtz says in this film. "What is falling should be pushed over," says the nihilist so accurately described by Nietzsche.

It is just for this reason that one has to conclude, finally, that unlove as such is not our rudimentary problem. It is not the first thing that has to be understood, unearthed, analysed, and if possible met by the redemptive word. It is there, of course: an enormous unlove, a violence of hatred surges through our civilization. But if we do not love, it is because we have not found a reason to love — because we have ceased finding the world worthy of love. In short, our sin is not first a matter of rejecting life but of finding life meaningless. It is despair, not unlove that first informs our way of being.

One could also point to distrust. It has by no means disappeared from the earth in our time! We trust very few people or things. Especially at the institutional level, a deep distrust informs the whole life of our society. After "Watergate," after "the October crisis," after thousands of broken promises between labour and management, after the repeated fall of governments in most countries of the Western world (and now in ours too) — who can one trust! Leadership has become an unbelievable concept. "Take me to your leader!" commands a creature from outer space of some bewildered earthlings. (What could "leader" mean?) A supposed leader is no sooner found and ensconced in office than he becomes the brunt of everyone's distrust and sarcasm. Our country is buzzing with jokes about political leaders. Most of them are not funny; they express enormous cynicism, not only about our leaders in particular, but all leaders. It might be asked whether any serious and sincere man or woman could be found to govern either the United States or Canada. Who would be trusted long enough? Distrust manifests itself at every level of our social fabric.

And yet it is not a *simple* distrust. It is not the same as the social distrust that informed the late Middle Ages — as Barbara Tuchman has so cleverly shown in her book *A Distant Mirror.*[34] Medieval humanity experienced a long period of distrust that was born of fear: fear of the plague, fear of the powers of secular and religious hierarchies that had become decadent and arbitrary, fear of starvation and perpetual war, fear of early death, fear of hell's fires — in other words fear of an apocalypse with judgment: God's judgment! Our distrust, rather, comes from the empty, lonely feeling that there is nothing behind it all to judge us, or them (the leaders, the institutions), or it (history, life). Ours is a complex distrust, born not of fear but of the experience of "the absurd": the sense of being all on our own in a universe that is entirely "indifferent" (Camus) to human destiny. The Medieval people couldn't trust their kings and archbishops because they thought their leaders had given up serving God. Contemporary humanity is enthralled by the suspicion that there are only . . . their leaders. That there is no transcendent Leader, no plan, no road map, no "inevitable progress," no kingdom — just whatever our unleaderlike leaders blunder into. Afterward the sociologists will tell us what we did. But nobody can be found to tell us what we *should do* — unless, of course, a public opinion poll can reveal clear-cut values! After that the political leaders certainly will be vocal!

While there is no need to disregard sin as unlove and distrust, it is necessary to acknowledge despair to have any great insight into the contemporary crisis. This has been the conclusion, not only of all the most sensitive theological reflection of our era, but of many other disciplines and analyses of the human condition as well — art in particular. All art, said Paul Tillich, can reflect three states of mind: hope, false hope, and hopelessess. He concluded, as a keen observer of contemporary graphic art in particular, that the dominant mood of art in our time is hopelessness. This applies to very much of the art in the Canadian scene today — especially literature.[35]

As for theology, it was not only that theological movement specifically designated "Theology of Hope" which has assessed the human condition in terms of the sin of despair. All responsible theology after the end of the nineteenth century (1 August

1914) has assumed that the fundamental condition that must be understood and addressed is the condition of despair. From the Theology of Crisis to present-day North American attempts at Liberation Theology, what the theologian and the church must reckon with as the primary manifestation of what is "wrong" with the world is the sense of meaninglessness, goal-less-ness, hopelessness which enshrouds our civilization and produces moods ranging from entire apathy to neurotic fear to the hedonistic pursuits of the Me Generation.

Thus, although the gospel still has to be addressed to the sin that is unlove and the sin that is distrust, it must be heard in a primary way as response to the Sin that is despair. Unless Christianity can speak to the various forms of despair in our contemporary world, it will not be *gospel* for that world, no matter how "right" it may be doctrinally. This is the point where the veracity of Christian faith must be tried today. The question of contemporary humanity is not first whether it is possible to love in a world of personal and corporate hatred, or whether it is possible to trust in a time of widespread cynicism, but whether it is possible to hope in an age which possesses no horizon of meaning beyond its own wishes and values. Where *this* question is not acknowledged, addressed, the majority will not be able to hear, in what Christians say, a gospel of love and justifying grace.

What would it mean to acknowledge and address the experience of sin as despair in the Canadian context?

3
Despair, Canadian Style

The Argument

Despair takes different forms. Where it has been open, as in Europe, Christian theology can respond by developing theologies of hope. In our society, theologies of hope are ineffective, because our form of despair is not open but hidden. Not wanting to face our corporate despair, anglophone Canada pursues the way of forgetfulness. But the repression of despair is only a temporary way of coping with reality.

The Differing Faces of Despair

We have said that it is the task of all responsible Christian theology today to *engage* despair. Throughout the contemporary world, especially the Western world, humanity has been seized by a failure of nerve. The dreams of the Modern epoch have given way to events and experiences which not only challenge those dreams, but which have thrown the dreamers into a state of crisis. Fallen from his high vision of a glorious future, man throughout the twentieth century has drifted toward despair. Theology must comprehend this despair and enter into dialogue and struggle with it. The best theology of our century has done just that.

But there is an important nuance here, and too much theology in North America particulary has missed this nuance — despair, like every other form of sin, has many faces. Despair may indeed be universal today, but it is by no means uniform. It does not assume the same shape everywhere. It can express itself very straightforwardly in melancholy, hopelessness, and cynicism, but it can also hide beneath smiling and laughter. It can be found in the minds of those who have no wish to camouflage it from the world, but it can also be deeply entrenched in the hearts of those who outwardly tell themselves and others a very different kind of story.

Anyone who wants to engage despair has to know what sort of despair he is dealing with. At bottom it may be that all the forms of despair are the same, but one cannot meet and struggle with one form by assuming that its characteristics are identical with another. For instance, if the despair in question is the kind that is disguised behind smiles and happy talk, it is useless to try to engage it the same way as the open sort expressed, say, in a novel of Marie-Claire Blais.[36] Here lies the reason why so much of our Canadian theology, having been hammered out on the anvils of European, South American, and other historical crises, is essentially inappropriate and ineffective in our context. For Canadian despair is different.

Something of the special character of our Canadian despair can be appreciated, I think, if we compare our situation with that of Europe. In the wake of wars which devastated the European continent, as well as an almost infinite number of economic depressions and social chaos of every variety, the great novels and plays of French and German authors in particular agonized openly over the loss of meaning widely felt in that society. Sartre's *Nausea* is perhaps the classical example; but the sickness of spirit, the apathy and nihilism which the twentieth century bred in the collective human soul of Europe, has been the characteristic feature of all the great imaginative writers of that continent from Dostoevsky and Kafka to Camus, Genet, Ionesco, Beckett, Grass, and many others.

European theology, especially after the second World War, was compelled to address itself directly to this situation, the situation of open despair. Theology became in the most immediate sense the engagement of despair in the development during the 1960s of a theological movement calling itself, straightforwardly, The Theology of Hope. The main spokesmen for this movement, Jürgen Moltmann and Johannes Metz, understood themselves to be speaking directly to a society which had been defeated and laid waste; a society, moreover, so fatalized by its own past that it was sure nothing really new could come to pass on the face of the earth. Particularly Germany — but much of Western Europe besides — had been exposed to systems which promised that all things would be made "new"; but instead they had inherited still more devastating forms of old chaos and evil. And in Eastern Europe the Modern dream, interpreted along the lines of doctrinaire Marxism, could be kept alive only through the suppression of alternatives by the Red Army.

To such a society, wallowing in the melancholy of the ages, the theologians of hope announced once more a gospel of "sheer grace": saying that God offers humanity possibilities which are not built into the historical process. True, according to our past we have no hope. We can expect nothing new, but only variations of old evils. But God has a future for us which is not strictly continuous with our past. From *his* future he offers us possibilities for renewal just at the point where *our* possibilities seem to have run out. At the edge of the Red Sea! So, combining Hebraic-Christian insight with concrete proposals for social transformation based on Marxist analysis (especially, in Moltmann's case, the neo Marxism of Ernst Bloch), the theologians of hope defined sin as the absence of hope and a consequent defeatism. To combat it they offered the miracle of a transcendent hope, of new possibilities introduced into the social structures by the God who will not leave his creatures in despair.

It is instructive to reflect on the fate of this Theology of Hope in our own society. It was, of course, eventually adopted. A slogan like "theology of hope" could hardly be resisted by a society and a church which always prided itself on thinking positively! But it was precisely as a slogan that it was picked up. It became the title of thousands of sermons in North America — preached, I suspect, by clergymen who usually didn't get beyond the first chapter of Moltmann's difficult book.[37] Besides, such a theme was somehow in keeping with the exuberant mood of the late 60s, and so it is not unusual that the theology of hope enjoyed a certain popularity among us for a time.

But the most interesting thing about this phenomenon is that it was so short-lived. Like the Death-of-God theological wave before it, the Theology of Hope gave way very soon to the next slogan, "liberation theology," which here and there still excites some Canadians. The reason for the brevity of this influence is not, I think, to be found primarily in our characteristically North Amerian habit of importing our theology ready-made from other people's crises, so much as in the fact that the Theology of Hope *was addressed to a form of despair that is not our own.* It was addressed to a European situation — a situation of quite transparent and openly-acknowledged anxiety. Just as we have never, in anglophone Canada, been able to identify with the "existentialist screaming" of novelists like Sartre and Camus, or the French Canadian writers like Blais and Langevin,[38] so we were not able to receive a theology which presupposes precisely the kind of despair made graphic by such novelists.

Covert Despair

The truth is, surely, that our particular style of social despair is much more complex than anything found on the left bank of the Seine. More subtle, too, than the anxiety patently acknowledged in French Canadian art and society. Our typical anglophone Canadian despair is a despair that is afraid of itself. The last word that it would choose to describe itself would be the word despair! Ours is a despair which unconsciously hides beneath its rhetorical opposite. It rarely or never gets to the surface of our thought. It is squelched by our collective consciousness before it reaches the level of reflection. Those in our midst who try to bring it to the surface and make us aware of it are regularly ignored. If they cannot be dismissed as exaggerators of the national condition (George Grant), or prophets of doom and gloom (many concerned ecologists), or political radicals (any number of people), then they are dismissed on the old, solid grounds of "immorality" (Margaret Laurence is a prime example). The

Cassandras of the Canadian landscape today are all, in one way and another, people who are trying to remind us of the underlying despair which, as a people, we do not want to hear about. Our despair is a covert thing, and we are trying desparately to keep it that way. It poses regularly under the guise of its opposite — optimism, positivism, hope!

Here lies the great dilemma of all theology that tries to take Canada seriously — that tries to be "contextual": How do you proclaim a gospel of hope to a society and church that daily assures itself and everyone around that it is already brim full of hope? How do you announce the impossible possibility of grace transcendent to a society that is unwilling and unable to recognize its own real despair? How do you speak about the possibility of the new (new life, the new creation) in a society which still calls itself "the new world," and where every television advertisement proclaims that the absolutely "new" is available this minute! Like every other society in the western world, our Canadian society too needs deliverance from a drifting to despair — needs a Theology of *Hope*! But how do you devise a Theology of Hope for an officially optimistic society: a society whose special form of despair manifests itself in its obsession with trivial forms of hope in order to repress its incipient awareness of its abysmal lack of authentic hope? If we are to speak of sin in Canada today, this is how we must learn to speak — not of immorality, not of private and public mistrust, not of obvious hatred, but of a secret and covert despair. It is a despair which does not and will not "know itself," which has no official existence. It reminds one of what Rolf Hochhuth causes his leading character, Winston Churchill, to say about the North Americans in his play, *Soldiers:* "Tragic — the word does not yet exist in America. They call it migraine."[39]

The word *despair* may not exist for us as a people, but the experience of despair is just beneath the surface of our consciousness. Our behaviour as a people betrays this in many ways. Some of these ways have already come into our reflections: the bewilderment of many (with George Grant) over Canada's apparent failure to seek an independent road into the future; the feeling of many of our most sensitive young people

— people who in other more expansive times would certainly have carved out a career in public life — that it is now time to leave the city of man and seek a more permanent place. Some, with Hugh MacLennan, have been drawn to nature.[40] Others find refuge in various old and new religions. It is covert despair also which provides the motor force for the great "internal immigration" that has come upon us, the Age of Aquarius having been succeeded by the Age of Narcissus. Meaning seems no longer linked to social and public causes; therefore many immigrate to the inner recesses of the self, to create the beautiful private world of the spirit within (transcendental meditation) or the body without (jogging).

It is our hidden despair as a people which shows through in the patent loss of national vision in anglophone Canada. We do not know who we are, or what we should become. We are possessed of a sentimental and often vociferous sense of the importance of "keeping Canada together"; but few amongst us can give profound or compelling reasons why this should be or what end it might serve. In the meantime, our actions — economic, cultural, educational and political — as well as our life style, our preferences in entertainment, our priorities in intangible values and tangible goods — all betray the fact that whatever national sentiments we may entertain at the rhetorical level, we gladly suppress them in order to keep hold of "the good life" as this has been defined for us by General Motors, General Electric, and Good Housekeeping Magazine!

Despair as Forgetfulness

Behind this drifting despair about the future there is (as one would expect there to be) a concommitant forgetfulness of anything in the past which might have helped us, as a people, to entertain a lively vision for ourselves and our children's children. It ought hardly to be necessary for Christians to remind one another that hope and remembrance are inextricably bound up with one another. We know, as those who remember Jesus in order to believe in his coming kingdom, what it means to look back in order to get ahead. Anglophone Canada no longer really cares to look back. Or let us say, to be more accurate, that its looking back is on the whole just as sentimental and as much inspired by hidden despair as is its rhetorical looking ahead. For real remembering it has substituted nostalgia. And even the superficial nostalgia of the world of antiques and historic sites cannot compete with the economic forces of our society which are capable of obliterating every shred of genuine evidence of the past. Not only do we trivialize the past by making it a commodity to be bought and used for decorative purposes, but for every historic plaque erected in this country there are a hundred more significant sentinels of our past which have been destroyed to make room for parking lots, high-rises, super-highways, and the like. In my own small-city birthplace in southwestern Ontario, there has been a constant battle for the past thirty years to prevent the demolition of its most ancient (and most beautiful) public buildings. The battle to save these buildings may not, in the ultimate scheme of things, be significant. Yet they do testify to a less tangible vision, and one cannot escape the impression that what the "progressive, commercial" forces of the city are really seeking to destroy, is that vision. For one thing, it frequently happens that the buildings they succeed in levelling are replaced by nothing at all, the "reasons" for the demolition notwithstanding.

It is in fact hard to remember what that vision was, even when one puts one's mind to it. In a way, as George Grant has said, all we have are "intimations of deprivation."[41] At fifty I have the vague impression that "something happened" — that between the world of my grandfather, who loved his land and his cattle, and my own generation, some vast and unnoticed transformation took place. The fact that my grandfather's farm is now owned by the Canada Cement Company is perhaps the best symbol of this impression. But sometimes the symbol is enlarged by imaginative art which can take us back to earlier times.

For example, Hugh MacLennan's "Captain Yardley" in *Two Solitudes*[42] seems to me to represent something of the vision that anglophone Canada has been busy forgetting. I think I can see my grandfather in this old Nova Scotia sea-captain, and also many others I have encountered across this country — persons in whom some remnants of the vision were retained. Captain Yardley is notorious for some things that he is strictly against: he has an innate suspicion of power, especially power coming from inherited wealth; he rejects the class structures which have been imported to North America from Britain and Europe; he despises the colonialized mentality and, along with it, all those who think the only acceptable way of being Canadian is to imitate the English; and he has an abiding suspicion of modernity, especially of technocratic forms of society and the loss of an immediate relation between man and the natural world.

But he is not just "against something"; he also stands for something. In fact, each of the things he dislikes are the negative side of what he likes and tries to live by: namely, an implicit democratic sense which insists that authority must be shared and special authority earned; the conviction of human equality which refuses to distinguish between persons on the basis of the accidents of birth and class and tongue; a feeling for the possibilities of the *Canadian* people, who therefore have no need to mimic the British; and a strong sense of belonging to nature (in his case, especially the sea) and of the stewardship of the natural world. Captain Yardley is a creation of fiction; yet in this figure MacLennan has captured something of the beginnings of a vision that once belonged to this country — not to its ruling elements, but to many others who, if they are not the "famous men" our history texts faintly praise, are the unsung multitudes who might have provided us with a different self-understanding had their memory been perpetuated: the sea-captains, the farmers, the fishermen, the adventurers, the settlers of the West, and countless others who were neither powerful nor articulate. It is not accidental that it was this same Captain Yardley in MacLennan's tale who, though he didn't even know the language, *found himself perfectly at home with French Canada!*

Perhaps more than any other feature of our Canadian anglophone society, the loss of the memory of such a vision betokens the real despair of our condition. And it seems to me very clear that if there is to be any genuine future for us as a people, it must entail something of the re-collection and reinstating of that vision. For the future and the past are never separable. We have lost something vital from our past, and our way into the future is handicapped without it. Memory and hope should not be regarded as incompatible moods. They are part of the same process — they are indeed "the same thing" (Paul Ricoeur). Far from being all future orientated, a society in which hope is really alive is at the same time a society caught up in the excitement of remembering. We do not have to be reminded of that in Canada today. For while we anglophone Canadians have been forgetting our better vision for the sake of a progress which did not materialize, the other Solitude has been busy remembering. *Je me souviens!* After a long and bleak winter of discontent, that other solitude has remembered with sufficient intensity that it has begun to hope.

A Wintertime People with a Summertime Fantasy

We have defined sin by reference to hope. Sin is hope's negation. It is despair.

What is the root of sin as despair? Sin as despair is, in part, the consequence of that in the human will which is not content with the creation as it is given us. It wills to create something greater, better, more perfect. It wills to fashion something from which all pain, paradox, uncertainty, all *crisis* is eliminated. From this restless will of mankind flows the grandeur of the species; but from it also flows our misery. We imagine — and we try to possess — a world from which the negative and negating dimension has been expelled; and this dream causes us to reject the world of our real experience, in which that negative element is still characteristically and often devastatingly present.

Modernity fashioned this ancient dream of the human race into a high ideal: pain would be eliminated, ignorance would be banished, the triumph of light over darkness would be achieved — the progress of history was assured. And this — this New World of North America — would be the place where it would happen first.

This fantasy carried greater weight in our sister country to the south than it was able to carry with us. We have tried very

hard to sustain this Modern myth of the already-redeemed creation. In our way we have tried to make this dream work. But
there are persistent realities that we have not, in the last
analysis, been able to escape: historical realties like our ethnic
diversity and our linguistic duality and our dependence upon
the founding and supporting empires by which we have been
moulded; natural realities like our vastness, our relatively
small areas of arable land, our insistent cold. Metaphorically it
could be stated in this way: We Canadians are a wintertime people with summertime fantasies.

And now is the winter of our discontent, because it has become so hard for us, in these bleak days, to blot out the fact that
our real habitat is winter. With all our artificial light and heat
we have come to the point where light and heat are running out
— literally and figuratively. Despite our attempts to escape our
wintry condition — our flights to Florida in the body and in the
spirit — the winter remains, and it seems to grow colder. Even
religion, that last human refuge against the cold, has lost its
warming power for great numbers of Canadians.

So one may ask: would it not, under such circumstances, be
appropriate for such a people to find the courage to live in the
winter? How might they exchange their false, ephemeral summer fantasies for a greater realism? How might they be persuaded
to stop trying to turn their world into perpetual summer and set-
tle, instead, for *winter* light?

II
"Winter Light"

4

The Nature and Test of Authentic Hope

The Argument

Against the condition of despair, we set the biblical concept of hope. Hope is sharply distinguished from certitude. It does not imply that the redeemed state is already realized, but suggests an openness to change. This distinction is important as we reflect on the Canadian situation. To speak about the overcoming of sin in our context would be both immodest and premature. As Canadians we shall have to go into our crisis more deeply before we can trust most expressions of its resolution. In the meantime, we may seek light — but it will be "winter light."

"Hoped For . . . Not Seen"

In a frequently quoted phrase from one of his best known poems, the nineteenth century Englishman, Shelley, asks —

> If Winter comes,
>   can Spring be far behind?

He means, of course, that our spirits should not flag in the dark days of our winter discontent, because all that will soon give way to the light and warmth of a spiritual springtime. As a nineteenth-century romantic (and not incidentally, a dweller in the moderate climate of England) he could well think so. But if you ask in the post-romantic, late twentieth century (and in Canada) whether if winter comes spring could possibly be far behind, you would expect a quite different answer!

To speak less parabolically: I think we should be cautious about becoming too enthusiastic over the signs of hope present in the Canadian situation. Our winter — our crisis — is still very much with us. Perhaps we are just entering its most serious phase. We have to live with its reality. Indeed, we shall have to come to terms with the harsh realities of our Canadian condition in a way that was not asked even of our pioneer ancestors. They had to face the bitter physical pain and deprivation of life in the forests and on the plains of this immense land. But they were given the courage to do so by the very qualities contemporary men and women have been deprived of — the sense, both social and religious, that they were carving out a New World here, free from the sins of the European fathers. We, their descendents, have begun to discover the truth of the biblical saying that "the sins of the fathers are visited unto the third and fourth generations." We have begun to realize that not even vast oceans and new beginnings can guarantee any essential discontinuity with the human past. Thus it is our destiny to confront a winter more bleak than that of our founding fathers and mothers: a spiritual winter brought on by the demise of the very dreams that kept them going.

In place, therefore, of Shelly's suggestion that the victory of spring over winter is imminent and inevitable, we may introduce a more appropriate metaphor around which to weave our reflections on hope: namely, the symbol of *winter light*. [43] What we may look for by way of "redemption" is like light given in the midst of winter. Not the great, soul-warming, overcoming light and warmth of spring — not yet! — but a little light in the midst of our winter.

This, in my view, is what it would mean to contemplate the Canada crisis from the perspective of that other, positive side of the Christian understanding of the human condition — redemption. Redemption for us as a people does not mean discovering immediate solutions to our critical condition, but finding sufficient intimations of hope to enable us to live within the crisis. To be conscious only of the danger side of the critical state is to be reduced to just that kind of despair we have been exploring: a despair which pretends that everything is all right when it isn't all right, a despair which says that it's summer when it's really winter! Hope means going far enough into the heart of the crisis to discern, now and then, its "possibility" side.

Possibilities are not inevitabilities. Hope, in the biblical meaning of the term, is to be sharply distinguished from certitude. "Faith," says the author of Hebrews (11:1) "is the substance of things *hoped for*, the evidence of things *not seen.*" Whatever Christian faith wants to say about the overcoming of sin, it must not be said in such a way as to imply that the sinful condition (the winter) is no longer our real condition (as if at this juncture of our discussion in Part II, we could speak as though everything said in Part I might now be set aside)! Certainly Christians have frequently behaved in that way. They have tried, often very pathetically, to persuade themselves and everyone else that now, having heard the gospel, having been "saved," the sinful condition has been entirely surpassed. Individualistic Christianity claims this kind of brand new existence for private faith. Liberal forms of Christianity, especially prior to the end of the nineteenth century, made similar claims for the whole "Christian" society. Instead of thinking in terms of hope and "possibilities," they thought along the lines of the realization of God's perfect kingdom here and now — often as if it were simply inevitable, a matter of social evolution.

Not only the Theology of Hope but all the great theological movements of this century have attempted, over against the kind of certitude informing both liberal and individualistic-conservative Christian views of redemption, to recover the biblical understanding of hope. The Christian message according to the Theology of Hope is not that evil, death, the demonic, and everything which negates life (the winter) has already been completely overcome — overcome in a way that is perfectly obvious, a matter of "sight"! Faith *does* posit an "already," but it is not the already of an obvious victory over that which distorts and destroys life. It is an already which sometimes becomes visible only to "the eyes of faith." Sometimes, in spite of the continuing reality of all that is implied in the word *sin*, there are intimations of the victory of God over sin. So far as ordinary experience ("sight") is concerned, this victory always seems a matter of anticipation rather than realization (a "not yet"). For "the victory of God is hidden beneath its opposite" (Luther). If it is perceived, it is not because it is terribly obvious, but because faith is granted the grace to "see" a deeper reality beneath the "obvious." "We do not see everything put beneath his feet," says the author of Hebrews, "but we see Jesus" (2:8) — we see the crucified one, who because he has identified with us in our suffering will conquer the cause of our suffering, and indeed has *already* done so. Glimpsing this hidden victory, faith is given the courage to live under the conditions of an existence which seems, for the most part, very much deprived of any dimension of victory. This faith does not expect redemption to be conspicuous. It does not expect summer in the midst of winter. Rather, it is kept going by intimations of hope — winter light. Because of this hope it is delivered from the fatalistic sense that nothing can be expected except infinite variations of what already is. Because of this hope it is able to entertain the prospect of significant change, even radical change. To entertain this not as if it were inevitable, necessary, built into the very scheme of things, but as *possibility*.

In other words, Christian hope walks the difficult but nevertheless traversible chalk-line between realism and idealism. Because of faith's refusal to substitute for the real world of everyday experience some "ideal" imagined or heavenly world, Christian hope must always avoid the premature optimism of most idealists. But because of faith's equally adamant refusal to believe that what can be "seen" in the world is all there is to be said about it, this hope must avoid the premature pessimism and fatalism of most of those who call themselves realists. Without turning its back on the data of despair, this faith tries to discern signs of hope. Without having to pretend that it is summer, this faith looks for light in the midst of the winter.

The Litmus Test of Hope

The characterization of Christian hope that I have given above, far from being a private interpretation, is something like a consensus of twentieth-century theology. Although there have been diverse emphases in the various movements and expressions of Christian theology during this century, they have all tried to translate the meaning of the gospel into forms of hope that were credible.[44] This was necessary, of course, because the earlier expressions of Christian eschatology had become *in*credible to the most representative and sensitive people of our time. "Orthodox" types of Christianity had either identified hope as already realized in the church or imminent, or both. Liberal Christianity, as we have seen, tried to translate the realization of God's purposes for creation into this-worldly terms, and thus found the kingdom of God just around the corner. Twentieth-century Christianity, wherever it has become genuinely aware of the age in which it finds itself, has realized that neither of these expressions of hope is credible. Not that everything about Christianity should be immediately accessible to the secular mind; but when past expressions of belief render the gospel especially inaccessible to ordinary human thought, then they must be rethought and replaced. After exposure to the wars and other characteristic events of this century, forms of hope which find God's purposes already realized in church or world are simply not accessible to human thought which wants to remain rooted in reality. Hence all the serious theological investigation of our era, from Barth's *Commentary on Romans* onwards, has been a search for the kind of articulation of Christian hope that does not have to shut its eyes to the data of despair in order to sustain itself.

When we come to speak about Canadian society from the perspective of that positive pole (redemption), we would do well to keep this general background of twentieth-century theologies of hope in mind. It will help to offset the influence of liberal and other expressions of redemption, which characteristically tend to overlook or downplay the data of despair in order to accentuate the positive side. But when the positive is achieved by suppressing or repressing the negative the result is inevitably cheap hope — in other words, an incredible expression of the ideal, which can be believed only by persons who are either unaware of the data of despair or, in keeping with our earlier discussion, looking desperately for ways of repressing what they know of that data. Incredible expressions of hope are bound to have a following in a society like ours. It staggers the mind to contemplate some of the highly "hopeful" and "positive" programs and schemes that people will latch onto in such a society — like drowning men grasping for straws! But Christians must not permit the gospel of Jesus Christ to be co-opted for these purposes. The litmus test of hope is not whether it can drum up a following, but whether those who follow are honest men and women with their feet firmly planted on the earth.

To have one's feet firmly planted on this Canadian earth at this juncture in history means one must especially be wary of cheap hope. It seems to me both necessary and good that at this point in our Canadian experience we must be more conscious of the negating dimensions of our corporate life than of the positive, cohesive side. I find myself, almost intuitively, distrusting anyone, Christian or otherwise, who comes forward with a blueprint for remedying our national sin! For example, I am usually made uneasy by liberal Christian talk about "reconciliation" between the two founding cultures of our society. This talk, for one thing, almost invariably originates from the side of the anglophone church and society, and it is always easy to speak about "reconciliation" when you are part of the majority. For another thing, such well-meaning counsel does not emerge out of a real struggle with and exposure to the deep manifestations of alienation between the Two Solitudes, and therefore it smacks of superficiality and false hope. It is the product of our summertime fantasies and not a result of exposure to the realities of our winter. Only those who enter far enough into the real alienation of our founding peoples from one another have, here and there, the right to begin to speak, modestly, about reconciliation. Naturally, being human, we want light! And our Enlightenment background taught us to look for light in which there was no shadow or turning. "More light!" cried the dying Goethe. Light is given, but it is winter light. The spring is not yet, and summer, for us, is a very elusive thing.

In other words, the criterion of authenticity for any form of hope is whether it gives evidence of having come to be in a conscious encounter with what would, and does, attempt to negate it. If what announces itself as hope does not know about the reasons why one should not hope, then it is false hope. Hope, in Christian terms, is always "hope against hope" (Romans 4) — as we have already heard from the young Barth. Hope is the courage to take up one's bed and walk in the face of years of paralysis. It is the apparent madness which goes forward at the edge of the Red Sea when no path appears in the waters. It is the determination to risk the possible that to all the world seems impossible. It is the foolishness of believing that human sin and absurdity have been decisively engaged, that history makes sense, that death itself will finally be beaten. But always this courage, this madness, this determination and folly — if it is really the offspring of Christian hope — must know what is and what it risks. It must know that it is a matter of *sheer grace*, not just of "thinking positively"; and it must know, too, that it risks being wrong, courting an illusion. To borrow a line from the profound American / Canadian philosopher Ernest Becker.[44a]

> The ideal critique of a faith must always be whether it embodies within itself the fundamental contradictions of the human paradox and yet is able to support them without fanaticism, sadism, and narcissism, but with openness and trust.

In other words, the credibility of our hope will be in direct proportion to its participation in the reality which causes our despair. On these grounds, the very act of beginning to think honestly about our condition — the very admission that we are a wintertime people — could be for Canadians a real token of hope. For only those who have been permitted to glimpse some signs of hope dare begin to *contemplate* the depths of their hopelessness.

The Advantages of Winter

Sometimes I am tempted to believe that there is a greater potentiality for such honest contemplation in this "true North strong and free" than can be found elsewhere on this continent, notably the United States. Insofar as that is so, it is more strictly a potentiality than a reality with us. Nor does it betoken any kind of superiority in us as a people. It is simply an accident of history and, more particularly, of nature — one of the advantages of winter that is regularly overlooked!

By this I mean that our very environment has prevented us from embracing, as heartily as we have evidently always wished to do, the bright, progressive world view in which the continent as a whole was shaped. That world view insisted that the human community, through rational technique and natural selection, was destined to master its environment and cause all creation to bow to its designs. But in comparison with the enormity of nature here, human society has seemed small, ephemeral, and weak. It is hard to stand out on the prairie, or by the sea, or in the midst of northern Ontario's myriad Christmas trees and think to oneself: "Man is the measure of all things!"

Perhaps our very smallness and relative weakness, the severity of our climate, the fact that the struggle for "survival" (Atwood) can be less easily glossed over here with the technological Good Life offered hourly by the television hucksters — perhaps nature herself has in some way prevented us from accepting that world view wholeheartedly. And to this may be added certain historical aspects of our culture: We were not so dramatically cut off from the older, European mother-cultures, which retained elements of Western humanity's pre-modern awareness of the tragic dimension of existence. In addition, we have received millions who have come to our shores later in time, who have been able for a longer period to maintain independent or semi-dependent communities, who therefore have not been so consistently swallowed up into the great monolith of the technological society but have kept some part of their former cultures, visions, folk-lore, and languages. Nor have we been able, in spite of our efforts, to subdue so thoroughly as our American neighbours have done, the indigenous peoples of this country; their voice still disturbs our peace and progress!

But above all, nature has inhibited us. Though we boast of our natural resources as if they were indeed ours, there is an aboriginal knowledge among us — the kind of awareness that precedes intellectual conditioning — of the fact that nature is bigger, more enduring, more relentless than we are. At a rudimentary level of consciousness we realize that we belong to nature, not she to us. We may and do inflict upon her own little designs and operations — some of them devastating enough; we may and do produce our James Bays and our Elliott Lakes. But the winter follows the autumn with regularity; and we know for all our hydro, uranium and natural gas projects that all that lies between us and the cold is a thin layer of technological "civilization." To the extent that this "gut" awareness has not been suppressed in us as a people (and I think it cannot be wholly suppressed), we have been prevented from becoming totally absorbed by the Modern positive outlook which promised to exchange winter for perpetual summer, sin for redemption here and now. Thus, as has been observed earlier in the discussion, we could never become "true believers" in the American Dream but could only produce a pale variant of the liberal vision of the Americans.

It should be repeated and underscored that this advantage — and at a time when the Modern vision is pathetically inadequate, it is an advantage not to have been accepted totally! — exists for us more as a potentiality than as something actualized in our public or private life. If it is there, it is at a very deep level of awareness and not at the level where decisions are made and plans laid. In fact it seldom surfaces except in the arts. At the level of consciousness, self-understanding and "value prioritizing," we are as much the children of modernity as that other larger nation of this continent. We are as enamoured as they of the technological society with its promises of a painless life and death. We are as victimized as they by a consumer culture which offers to lift man well above the level of nature to ever greater heights of mastery and pleasure. We are just as keen as they to visit the Disney World, to confirm our desperate wish that the real world would behave like that too.

Nevertheless there is a certain advantage to our winter. For every world view must finally be tried on the anvil of nature. I have said that the test of hope is whether those who profess it keep their feet solidly planted on earth. The Christian does not ask of systems of meaning and hope that they conform to nature at every point; for Spirit can evoke from nature that which nature itself cannot produce. But systems of meaning and hope which cannot stand the most basic tests of the natural world cannot for long entice those who are most vulnerable to nature. The Modern world view promised far more to humanity than it could finally deliver. Europeans through their turbulent contemporary history made this discovery long before anyone on this continent. But while nature may not be so effective or so quick as history in providing lessons for slow-learning human beings, she is sure in the longrun. She will not tolerate human projects and ideals which entice the spirit but forget the body. With its vision of perpetual summer, modernity lured gullible, spiritual humanity to the edge of the abyss. But those most vulnerable to nature (notably, the poor) have never been the chief exponents of that vision. To the extent that Canadians share that vulnerability (and the Captain Yardleys do), there is a certain basis in our *physical* condition for the more nebulous and spiritual "intimations of hope" I shall try now to convoke.

5
Intimations of Hope in Canadian Society

The Argument

There are certain emergent realities in present-day Canadian society which Christians may regard as signs of hope. Among them we discuss in particular the emergence in French Canada of a people which "remembers," as well as various protesting and resisting minorities which seek alternative forms of human community. Such movements point toward the possibility of social transformation; the extent to which the possibility is actualized will depend largely on the character of the support they can find.

Je me souviens!

Using the criteria for authenticity we have discussed in the foregoing chapter, we may ask now for concrete evidence of hope in the contemporary Canadian scene. We have considered the danger side of our crisis. What may we now discern on the side of possibility?

It goes without saying that in such a brief discussion as this it is not possible to treat everything which could be brought forth as evidence. Instead, I shall concentrate on such intimations of hope as can further elaborate the kind of hope that Christians, in my view, find provocative. Therefore I shall not be discussing such things as the prospect of greater oil and gas deposits being discovered beneath the crust of Canada, or more advantageous trade arrangements being worked out with the European Common Market or the Chinese, or the growth of the Gross National Product. These and similar prospects are no doubt seen as hopeful possibilities by all those who believe that we must maintain at all costs our present standard-of-living — and better it! But as a Christian and a humanist I do not find this either a realistic or a desirable future; for one thing, it is a future which could be acquired by Canada only at the expense of many others in God's beloved world. I look, rather, to emergent realities in our society which contain, in embryo, a quite different vision and role for our land.

Among such realities the one which seems to me the most conspicuous is the emergence in French Canada of a people whose "remembering" has at last articulated itself in an astonishing mood of hope. That this most conspicuous and dramatic intimation of hope is also the most consistently misunderstood and misconstrued is all the more reason for treating it first.

It is not necessary to become romantic about Québec, or to gloss over the inconsistencies and problems of its present government, to realize that something very hopeful is happening here, and to admire it. This is a real hope. It passes the litmus test to which I have referred, for it has come to be out of a stark and even bitter encounter with its antithesis. It is not sheer idealism, but understands itself to be "winter light." Francophone Canadians have had an awareness of their "winter" in a way that only a small minority of anglophone Canadians have had. There are of course linguistic, economic, political, and ecclesiastical reasons for this. English is the language of "success" in North America, and it did not take great imagination or insight for ordinary French Canadians to perceive that their language was being gradually but surely eroded. And of course language is only one dimension of the erosion, though in many ways it is the most conspicuous dimension. What was occurring at the linguistic level was reflected in the more complex realms of economics, politics and culture at large. A church which still counselled its folk to seek their hope in the heavenly kingdom did not find it seriously necessary to resist the oppressive forces which were eating away at French Canadian society. But in the post-War decades particularly, Québec became conscious of its own debilitating despair, to which its artists, novelists, playwrights, and musicians gave poignant expression. Tales like those told in *Thirty Acres, The Tin Flute, Dust Over the City,* and *A Season in the Life of Emmanuel,* articulate an almost unrelieved despondency.

Out of this despair, combined with the remembering of a very different past, a society no longer content to wait for heaven's consolations gradually began to transfer to earth pieces of the dream inherited from its religious traditions. No doubt some of the versions of the dream that has emerged are extravagant. No doubt the dream has here and there taken the nasty turn of becoming a programatic and inflexible ideology. But we should not mistake what is really happening in all of this. It is a rebirth of hope, through a renewal and reworking of what is remembered.

The pathetic, even tragic, thing about these eventualities is that the majority of anglophone Canadians within and outside Québec do not see the positive side. Instead of perceiving the rebirth of hope in a people, Anglo-Canadians with few exceptions experience this as a resurgence of blatant, obsolescent, and destructive nationalism.

It is just this that prevents what is hope for Québec from becoming a sign of hope for Canada. The onus is on Anglo-Canadians to reverse this situation. Our choice is: either we can continue simply to resent and resist Québec's aspirations, or we can be inspired by French Canada to seek new aspirations of our own. What is occurring in Québec can be thought a sign of hope for Canada only if we choose the latter alternative.

A few of us have come close enough to French Canada to look beyond our own feelings of insecurity in the face of all this, and to begin to sense what is happening in this other ''solitude.'' We have felt the excitement of a people which, on the very brink of disintegration, has found the courage to become a people again. Christians among us have been caused by this experience to remember certain biblical parallels. We have come to think that what is astonishing in the Canadian scene today is not, after all, the fact that French Canada seems to have found the courage to resist the encroachment of "the universal and homogenous state" (Grant), the mass culture which is reducing us all to a common denominator of human mediocrity; rather, it is that English-speaking Canadians seem to allow their culture, whatever distinctiveness, uniqueness, memory, and vision it may once have had, to disappear with hardly a trace of regret!

Consequently we find ourselves in a strange position. While for Christian or simply human reasons we are opposed to Québec 'separatism', we are able sincerely to empathize with Québec nationalists who fear that unless Québec achieves autonomy, its alternative vision will suffer the same fate as did the embryonic vision once (tentatively, precariously) present in Anglo-Canadian society — in the Captain Yardleys. The best challenge to anglophone Canada that I have ever read comes from the voice of the most vociferous separatist in Québec today, Pierre Bourgault, who exhorts English-speaking Canadians to build a country —

> Maybe you'll build something attractive enough for us to want to compromise and give up the thought of having a country of our own. Be creative — build your own identity. Don't waste your energies bulldozing ours. Start believing in yourselves, and then maybe we'll believe in you, too. The day you believe in Canada as much as I believe in Quebec, 90 percent of our problems will go away, because then — and only then — two proud peoples will be able to face each other on an equal basis.[45]

The Task Force on Canadian Unity seems in basic agreement with this challenge.

The problem is not French Canadian remembering; it is English Canadian forgetting. Our peculiar despair expresses itself, as we have observed earlier, in forgetfulness. The past cannot teach us all that we need to know for the future. But without remembering some of our greatest moments, symbols, and dreamers we shall have no criteria for discerning the meaning of the present, and no firm building-materials for constructing the future. It is not, I think, that Anglo-Canada has nothing to remember. It is rather that our more provocative past — the past represented by the seamen, farmers, railroad workers, and lumbermen, by many of our artists and literary figures, and by some of our statesmen, clergy, and professional men and women — that this past was too soon and too thoroughly snatched away from us by the dominant business interests and classes which promised us, in its place, instant summer. We could learn from Québec and French Canada the formula for hoping. It is not an easy road. But it is better than oblivion.

Protest, Resistance, Search

As a second sort of winter light, we may consider a great variety of movements, groups, and causes which I would bring together under the title of "a protesting minority." By comparison with the 1960s this segment of our society may seem less impressive now. Perhaps it really is, or perhaps it has simply become, more integrated and less noisy. In any case, by comparison with other periods in our recent history, this minority still has political and religious significance. There has always been a protest movement in Canada — usually more than one. But I think that the dimension of protest, resistance against the status quo and the search for alternatives is greater in our present society and during the past two decades than formerly.

It is of course also more diverse. And it is no secret that the diversity of the protesting element is counterproductive. Protest movements have always been notorious for their inability to co-operate. They are usually too dependent upon having a conspicuous common enemy. No doubt the reason why the protest movement can seem less inspiring today than it was in the 60s is chiefly because of the fact that, then, "the enemy" was much more obvious. It was visible as the polluter of our lakes and rivers and as American aggression in Viet Nam. Eventually it even found a face: Richard Nixon. Today it is hard to identify the enemy, and the spirit of protest is consequently both less precise and less integrated, yet it has not dissipated altogether,

and some suggest that it will shortly come into a new prominence.[46]

The reason why I group together this great variety of causes
and persons is that in spite of differing expressions and motiva-
tions, they all represent a resistance against the dominant
culture, its values, its direction, and the search for alternatives.
It is particularly important for Christians to reflect on what is
happening in and through these diverse causes and movements,
because what we must finally ask ourselves is whether such a
thing may be said of our "movement," too. Does the Christian
movement also contain a prophetic protest against the spirit of
our dominant culture? Does it, too, stand as an alternative? Can
it also, therefore, join forces here and there with these others
who protest, resist, and search? Or does the Christian church
exist chiefly to confirm and uphold the established order — the
order of a society which despairs but will not admit of despair.

The general framework of analysis that we may use for this
reflection on the protesting minority is one which has been suggested very often during the last century or so, in a number of
different forms. The form I find most useful is one articulated by
Paul Tillich. In an insightful essay called, "Aspects of a
Religious Analysis of Culture,"[47] Tillich described contemporary Western civilization in terms of two contending social
forces.

> Our present culture must be described in terms of one pre-
> dominant movement and an increasingly powerful protest
> against this movement. The spirit of the predominant move-
> ment is the spirit of industrial society. The spirit of the pro-
> test is the spirit of the existentialist analysis of man's actual
> predicament.

What Tillich means by "the spirit of industrial society" is
similar to what more doctrinaire socialists than he mean by
"capitalism"; and it bears considerable resemblance also to
what a great variety of more recent commentators (Jacques
Ellul, George Grant, Philip Slater, Garrett Hardin and others)
mean by "the technological society" or "technocracy." The
two primary thrusts operative in this dominant cultural force,

Tillich claims, are: (1) the ''methodological investigation and technical transformation of [the] world [and mankind] and the consequent loss of the dimension of depth in [our] encounter with reality;'' (2) the belief that man is autonomously capable of mastering the universe.

Against this dominant spirit of society, Tillich identifies ''existentialism'' as the protesting element. In this I think he demonstrates his essentially European orientation. There can be no doubt that French and German existentialism has contained a clear expression of the protest against the manipulation of nature and humanity through the technocratic application of rationality. There may be no more blatant rejection of the spirit of modern technocracy than Heidegger's essay on thinking.[48] Also, interestingly enough, the imaginative literature of French Canada has much in common with existentialism in this connection.[49] But it would be wrong to identify the protesting minority in North America generally, and in Canada particularly, with existentialism — or, for that matter, with any aspect whatsoever of professional philosophy or academic inquiry. Perhaps it would have been better for us if we had some leadership from such a purposive and theoretically calculated movement. But as it has happened — characteristically enough for this New World — the protest against the spirit of the technological society here has been, and is, far more practical and less theoretically pure, more 'hit-and-miss' than in Europe and, ironically, frequently more effective.

I would identify this protesting minority with three types of activity, which we may for purposes of identification name *political, environmental,* and *artistic* activity.

(i) *Political*[50]: If you have lived in the United States, and also in Saskatchewan and Québec, as I have done, then you cannot help realizing something very significant about Canada — at least about parts of it (and, I would say, potentially of the whole): namely, that it is possible in this country to embrace not only a different political platform but a different social vision from the dominant one — and to do so within the structures of our political system. It may seem like blatant party politics to make such a statement; nevertheless it belongs to a discussion of this nature. After all, a society in which it is not possible to identify at the level of party politics with a segment of the society which dreams a different dream, but only with variations of the same basic social concept, lacks an important ingredient of hope — the possibility of a viable public alternative to the status quo, the possibility of radical change through democratic process.

Nor should one jump to the conclusion that such a claim constitutes a not-very-indirect endorsement of the political Left. It is true that the socialist alternative is the dimension of our political scene in Canada which most distinguishes us from our American neighbour. It is also true that the political Left has been the most consistent dreamer of a different sort of dream. But there have been and are great visionaries on the Right also in our history; for with us Conservatism has not always been synonymous with reaction or the maintenance of the vested interests of the upper classes. It has existed, often, as a protest against the dominant, "Liberal Idea of Canada";[51] and at its best, it has been inspired by that very remembering which I have identified as the missing background for hope in Anglo-Canadian society.[52]

In short, protest, resistance, and the search for alternatives have been possible in Canada at the level of politics — and in a way that seems to me truly rare in the history of the human race. For all its practical ambiguity, Christians ought to regard this as an intimation of hope.

(ii) *Environmental:* The past two decades have seen the emergence of something which could hardly have been prophesied prior to the end of World War II. For the first time since its rise to prominence and power in the Western world, the scientific community (through a significant minority of its membership) has given clear indication that it is not and does not wish to be the inspirer and servant of the spirit of industrial society. Heretofore there were, to be sure, individual scientists who saw their rôle in society in prophetic, protesting terms, but that has not been the attitude of the natural sciences on the whole. Today, when there are many scientists who speak out against the direction of the dominant technocratic society, and when these voices are allowed to be heard even in high places, it should not be forgotten that this is a quite new phenomenon. Prior to the 1960s, when the crisis of the biosphere became too horrendous to repress any longer, the scientific community were for the most part apt to echo the sentiment of the great Oppenheimer, who said, "If the experiment is sweet, then we must pursue it." Nor should we overlook the fact that the bulk of science is still in the employ of the dominant industrial society. It is said that in the United States no less than 51% of all scientists work directly in the service of death, especially relating to defence. Yet it is a matter of almost singular hope to those humanists and others who have protested the industrial-technical mentality for more than a century, that they are joined today by representatives of the very genius of humanity that gave rise to the industrial society.

Something else that should be noticed in connection with the scientific protest and the hope implicit in it for a still-habitable earth is this: its most profound spokesmen are more concerned to bring us into the awareness of the *problem* than they are to put themselves forward as its solvers. This is frustrating to many, but on the grounds of the criteria for authentic hope that we have established here, this must be regarded precisely as an intimation of legitimate hope. It is tempting for science and technology to mouth the optimistic credo of their sponsoring society, and to offer instant solutions to all our problems, but nothing is to be feared more today than the solutions of people who do not know the depths of the problem. It is a mark not only of a new and commendable modesty in science but of something like an intuitive recognition of the litmus test of hope to which I have referred, that so many scientists are saying: It is the *problem* that we have to try to understand! This new science wants to make sure that it has gone deeply enough into the *problematique*, which is extremely complex, before it shows up as problem-solver. In the language of our metaphor, it is content with winter light.

Here, for example, is the statement of an ecologist introducing a recent study. Fully aware that his readers expect him to provide answers, he writes:

This work is designed to show that [North American] political values and institutions are grossly maladapted to the era of ecological scarcity that has already begun. It is thus almost entirely a critique . . . . I make no systematic effort to provide institutional answers . . . .

This has distressed many readers of this work in manuscript. Like most . . . they appear to find a discussion of problems that offered no definite solutions — much less ones that could be called 'feasible' or 'realistic' . . . rather unsettling. . . .

However, the value of the present work lies in the nature and quality of the questions it raises. . . . Until we have these questions clearly in mind, their answers are bound to elude us.[53]

Such an approach, in my view, betokens far more genuine hope than all the advertisements of the Ford Motor Company which continue to assure us that if technology created some problems, it can also solve them.

(iii) *Artistic:* If the delineation of the elusive character of our despair is a prerequisite of the process of hoping (as I have insisted it is), then none of the protesting elements in our Canadian society have been so insightful as have our own artists. We could speak here at length about the graphic artists: the famous Group of Seven, whose work has been largely monopolized by the dominant bourgeois culture, was trying to tell us something about the character of our winter. And the Maritime artist, Alex Colville, who is regarded by many today as the greatest realist painter in the world, poignantly depicts the victory of the plastic world of technique over the natural and spontaneously human.

The more direct art, that of imaginative writing, has been almost tireless in its attempt to help us look at ourselves without the benefits of the rose coloured glasses and summertime fantasies provided by our official philosophy and its commercial backers. Anyone who read and understood Sinclair Ross's *Lamp at Noon* or Margaret Laurence's *The Fire Dwellers* would not have to wait to be told by social scientists that we are a people harbouring a secret, repressed despair, and living in a protracted state of crisis. This has been in fact the almost universal message of our artists. In this respect, Anglo-Canadian writers and artists do not differ greatly from their French Canadian or European counterparts, who depict the Modern world torn between hopelessness and false hope.

The Anglo-Canadian writers, however, have been remarkably true to that special type of despair that belongs to us as a people: the type that poses as optimism and says that it is always summer. Very often (to anticipate the next chapter in our study) this repressed despair uses the symbolism of the Christian religion to achieve its goal. In many Canadian novels, therefore, the connection between religion and repression is a recurring theme. The following, cutting passage from Margaret Laurence's *A Jest of God* is typical:

> The wood in this church is beautifully finished. Nothing ornate — heaven forbid. The congregation has good taste. Simple furnishings, but the grain of the wood shows deeply brown-gold, and at the front, where the high altar would be if this had been a church which paid court to high altars, a stained-glass window shows a pretty and clean-cut Jesus expiring gently and with absolutely no inconvenience, no gore, no pain, just this nice and slightly effeminate insurance salesman who, somewhat incongruously, happens to be clad in a toga, holding his arms languidly up to something which might in other circumstances have been a cross. [54]

Hope, we have said, is a dialogue with despair. By that criterion, the artistic community of Canada has perhaps been more faithful in its search for genuine forms of hope than those who make it their business.

Where are the Midwives?

To these movements of protest, resistance, and the search for alternatives others could be added: the attempt to keep minority cultures from disappearing, the various quests for educational alternatives, the search for sexual equality, the struggle for the rights and dignity of our indigenous peoples. All such move-ments represent possibilities of transformation. That they are often ambiguous, impure, or fragmented does not alter the fact that they stand for something different and "new". Hope always strains for what is new (even though it may also be very old), because it depends upon the prospect of altering "what is". Hope for Canada, for all its specificity, is not different in that respect. It too strains towards the new: a new society, a new relation between humanity and nature, new relationships bet-ween men and women, between citizens and government. These movements in our midst are fragments of a new vision which is trying to be born.

It is not a foregone conclusion that that vision will ever come into being, or even that there will be approximations of it. For every new thing that is born there must be pain, and there must be midwives. Canadians have been seduced by a way of life that promises to be pain-free, and we resent the pain this new vision and its representatives continually cause us. But beyond that, we seem deplorably short of midwives — of those who care enough for "the new" to help give it birth, of those who are skilled enough in giving birth to support those in whom some fragment of hope is waiting.

What about the Christians? The church has a reputation, de-served or not, for caring. Can the church in Canada take up the role of midwife to hope?

6
The Crisis and
the Churches

The Argument

Prophetic faith believes that God is at work in the midst of historical crises. The church is called not so much to do God's work as to recognize it wherever it is happening, to make common cause with those through whom it is happening, and to help it happen. Here and there in Canada today, some such concept of the church is manifesting itself. But it is greatly inhibited by lingering conventions stemming from a different model of the church. If we are to explore the possibilities of prophetic ministry in the church today (the intention of the final chapter), we must first be honest about those inhibiting factors.

"God Moves in a Mysterious Way . . ."

Following the Task Force on Unity and many other recent analyses, we have been reflecting on Canada using the language of crisis. The whole human race has been experiencing a profoundly critical period throughout the present century, notably during these latter decades — after Auschwitz, after Hiroshima. In some ways the crisis is particularly acute in the so-called Western world; for being the cutting-edge of the modern world view, and seeming so firmly established in that vision, the Western world is especially unsettled by the questions that history has put to modernity. The Canada crisis is a participation — a particular sort of participation — in the critical transition through which Western civilization is passing.

There is a mystery at the heart of historical crises which human wisdom cannot fathom. Certainly we may observe many things about such critical periods as they have occurred throughout history, and make generalizations concerning them. Evidently such periods occur at the point where the assumptions, expectations, goals, and mores of a society no longer seem adequate or true — where the fundamental vision informing that culture is no longer sustained by experience. There is a "shaking of the foundations." The old world view doesn't work any longer, and one is not sure whether anything can be found to replace it. But why doesn't it work?

Christians, if they are appropriately modest about their own capacity for wisdom, will not claim that they can understand this mystery. Yet they are bound to make the attempt to relate what is happening in the world to their belief in a God who loves and wills to redeem the world. Therefore they cannot regard apparent evil in the world — including foundation-shaking crises which threaten whole civilizations — as if it were purely accidental, or the result only of human error or sin or the demonic. All historical crises no doubt contain a good deal of the accidental, erroneous, sinful, and demonic. Yet if God is Lord of history and wills to redeem his creation, then he must somehow be involved in the whole process — including the crises. Moreover, while the mystery of his involvement is unfathomable, biblical faith never regards it as merely capricious or irrational. The divine love *(agape)* may indeed be "spontaneous and unmotivated" (Nygren), but it is not without reason. To the humanly wise God's wisdom may indeed seem foolishness (I Cor. 1-2), but that is largely because God's wisdom is generated by love and not (as human wisdom regularly is) by the quest for power.

In this connection it is instructive to meditate on the etymological and biblical connotations of the word *crisis*. We have already noticed that it has to do with decision, for it stems from the verb *krino* — to decide. There is a turning point, and we are called to decide which way we will go. But biblical faith knows also about another aspect of this Greek word. The noun *krisis*, from which our word *crisis* directly derives, means judgment. In the scriptures this is the word usually used to refer to God's judgment. God's judgment is not only that last judgment which is still awaited, but a *krisis* which is continuously being introduced into the historical process. The judging, loving God enters into critical confrontation with individual and corporate humanity, struggling against the "inevitabilities" introduced into the historical process by the arrogant and slothful spirit of humanity.

As this word-study already suggests, prophetic biblical faith views human, historical crises (for example, the expulsion of Israel from Egypt, the Babylonian captivity of Israel, the persecution of the first Christians) as manifestations of the party hidden, partly revealed *krisis* of the loving God. Far from being beyond the will of God, the crisis is seen by faith as a working-out of God's will for his people.

In the spirit of this prophetic tradition, twentieth-century Christian thought from the Theology of Crisis to present-day Liberation Theology has attempted to interpret the crisis of Modern Western civilization in the light of this image of God as the one who must judge because he loves. God is in the midst of the crisis, it has declared. Crisis is not merely the result of a weakening of human self-confidence, nor is it merely the result of the "inevitable" breakdown of the capitalist society. It is a consequence of the love of God, who must judge what he loves in order to save his beloved world from self-destruction. If the foundations are shaking, it is because they are the wrong foundations. If our expectations are no longer upheld by our experience, it is because they are the wrong expectations. If our values no longer find any basis in objective reality, it is because they are the wrong values. If nature no longer supports our view of the world, it is because our view of the world is questionable. God is "at work in the world, making and keeping human life human" (Paul Lehmann) — and therefore he will not leave intact anything that dehumanizes humanity, especially its own outmoded world views. God cannot override or simply suppress the thoughts and works of humanity, even when they are self-destructive or inappropriate; for he will have human beings who are free, who respond in love to love offered. But he will nevertheless struggle with our proud empires; and against our will-to-power, our irresponsibility, and our violence he will bring his loving judgment. *For* us he will strive *against* us. And always in his rejection of the old, he will be offering the new.

This is the meaning of crisis as a theological category, as distinct from purely historical or sociological reflection.

Discipleship as Midwifery

The task and calling of the church must be seen in relation to the theological meaning of historical crises. If from the human side crisis implies the need for decision, and from the side of the gospel it refers to the mysterious operations of divine grace, then we may say that the task of the church is to help mankind perceive the grace hidden in its crises and to decide for the new that is being offered through the judgment of the old.

It is not the task of the church to provide this possibility, this grace — as if in the first place it were capable of doing any such thing. It does not have to provide anything at all, except the imagination to recognize grace when it meets it on the street! Even that imagination — according to the New Testament's concept of the Holy Spirit — is a gift. If God is himself "at work in the world, making and keeping human life human," and if his movement in history is always "mysterious," then it will be quite enough for the church, if it can have the wit and freedom from its own past conventions, to be able sometimes to recognize God's humanizing work.

This suggests a very different concept of Christian obedience than the one which has dominated most historic forms of Christendom, especially since Christianity ceased thinking of itself as "salt" and "yeast," "seed" and "candle," and began to apply to itself the language of grandeur: "Like a mighty army moves the church of God." Contemporary theology does not apologize for this change; for it finds the earlier, biblical metaphors not only more in keeping with the real (sociological) condition of the church today but also more appropriate theologically.

In the religiously pluralistic society, the church can no longer
pretend to be the only representative of God and the only doer of
his will without inviting scorn. More important, it does not
have to indulge in this fiction any longer; for it can find in its
own best traditions, as well as in much of its present experience,
the courage to believe that God has not abandoned his world but
is at work, in mysterious ways, even in its deepest crises. It is
able to think of itself therefore no longer as "army" but in the
more modest terms of the midwife. Keeping its eyes open and its
presuppositions carefully in check, the community of disciples
watches history for the evidences of God's labour. There is pain
in this labour, as in all birth-giving. But it is a pain which can be
entered into with some rejoicing on account of the new thing
that is coming to be. Awake and alert the midwife listens for the
sounds and watches for the signs she half remembers — for
every birth is new. At the critical hour she is tense, expectant,
and afraid that it will not go well.

To compare the church to the midwife is to take from her that
other role to which she has clung throughout the centuries:
mother! Here the mother is no longer the church herself, but the
world. It is the world with which God strives to bring forth the
new humanity, the new creation. No doubt the image of the
mother church has some historical validity and some continuing
symbolic meaning. But it is so inextricably bound up with the
church's matriarchal bid for power that it is very difficult to
redeem the image for meaningful use. We should return rather
to the pre-Constantinian concept of Mary the Virgin as representative of humanity, and more particularly that representative humanity called Israel. The imperial church took over
the symbol of the mother for itself, for it knew the potency of
that symbol! It is the world which God impregnates with his
eternal seed. It is history which he beckons towards a gracious
end. It is humanity he wills to transform through the Spirit of
his Son. The church is present only as midwife, to recognize
what and where and through whom this new thing is to come.

That is why it is so important, in the crises of human history,
that the church should pay particular attention to the protesting
minorities such as those to which we have drawn attention in

the previous chapter. For if the experience of Israel and prophetic Christianity can be trusted, it is precisely in and through
these minorities that the new / old humanizing work of God is
seeking another entrée into human history. Of course God's
work cannot be identified unqualifiedly with their specific alternatives! Of course there are ambiguities and dangers of every
kind in what these political, environmental, artistic, sexual,
racial, and other alternatives stand for! No human movement
can be said to express perfectly God's will for his world. But in
their struggle against the old, oppressive forms of society, in
their resistance against a status quo which guarantees the
affluence of a few at the expense of the many, in their search for
a way into the future, these minorities taken together give con-
creteness to the hope that there can be something new under the
sun after all. They represent in specific and often poignant ways
the birth pangs of the new creation. Without intending it, they
can be perceived as "mother" of possibilities for a human future
yet untried — a mother having very much in common with that
one whose name means "bitter myrrh," including a basic incapacity for such a birth!

The theological significance of the protesting, resisting,
searching minority in our time, and in Canada in particular,
should not be underestimated. But again we ask: Is the church
capable of midwifery? Are the churches able to respond in the
critical hour?

Barriers to Obedience

We may answer at once that a significant number of Christian
individuals and smaller groups, and even some denominations
at the level of certain aspects of their official policy, have
declared themselves in word and deed to be ready to work out of
such a model of the Christian community. In areas such as
native peoples' causes (Project North), intercommunity of
anglophone and francophone Christians (Dialogue), solidarity
with the world's hungry (Ten Days for World Development),
concern over energy and lifestyles (Project Ploughshares) and in
many other ways, Canadian Christians and churches have

begun to explore the kind of image of the church which theologians and others have been elaborating: the diaspora, the Christian minority, the church as witnessing community, as midwife. But before we shall be able to further and foster that image, we must become more articulately aware of the forces within our own lives as churches which inhibit and retard the emerging of such an image.

First, we have inherited a strong convention of Christian *otherworldliness* which finds the whole attempt to locate hope within historical existence questionable. Whatever many of us may feel about the this-worldly orientation of the Christian message, we should not overlook the fact that a very large percentage of Canadian Christians are moved by another gospel altogether, which counsels them to be suspicious of every attempt to implement the promises of Jesus in this present world. Even asking specifically about Canada and the Canada crisis constitutes for this mentality a kind of betrayal of the gospel, or an exchange of eternal truth for humanistic concerns. While this attitude is not as adamant in the main line denominations as in the growing sectarian movements, it is one from which few of us can entirely free ourselves.

Second, another extremely powerful thrust within the kind of Christianity which is historically and currently influencial in our society is its *privatism.* Many Christians who would not be altogether non-worldly in their religion nevertheless do not open themselves to the prospect that Christian hope should inform society. Hope is for the soul — or perhaps for the religious community, the church. The idea that Christian hope should somehow express itself in social, political, and economic terms either does not occur to this type of Christianity or is repudiated by it. This is perhaps an even more devastating deterrent to the kind of hope we have been thinking about here, because again today as at some other moments in our history, there is a strong movement towards private religion. The age of Narcissus knows very well how to express itself in Christian terms, just as it knows how to pursue the narcissistic cult of the body.

Third, all forms of Christianity (even the most nonconformist) are the inheritors of that subtle but insistent *Chris-*

tian imperialism which always wants to be in the lead. It may not renounce the idea of hope for society, but it wants to be the chief if not the exclusive purveyor of hope. It is extremely hard for many Christians to entertain the notion that, in the post-Constantinian world, the forms of hope that may emerge may not be duly labelled Christian or even religious; they may in fact be introduced by persons and movements avowedly anti-Christian! It is however true, not only in Latin America, Asia, and Europe but also in Canada (which is fast becoming religiously pluralistic in a conspicuous way), that it is possible to speak realistically about hope for our society only if we are prepared, as Christians, to hear this hope articulated in terms which are often quite different-sounding — different from anything heretofore advanced under the aegis of Christ. There can be no question of an exclusively Christian programme of social hope. Besides, as we ought to have learned from our own scriptures, the providence of God towards suffering humanity has hardly ever come in a direct way, through people who announced themselves on earth as his representatives. The task of the church is not to manufacture the hope but, as we have said above, to recognize its signs and help it come to pass. And that is not a rôle to which sixteen centuries of Christian exclusiveness has conditioned us!

Fourth, there is an even more complex deterrent to Christian participation in the labour of hope. Far more insidious than the sort of blatant Christian imperialism which wants to have exclusive rights to the formula for hope is that perennial Christian *theological triumphalism* — compounded in our North American churches by its combination with New World optimism — which wants to have the hope without any deep or lasting vestige of its antithesis. It does not want to dialogue with despair, but to vanquish it once and for all. This same triumphalism has dominated Christianity ever since it sold its Hebraic birthright for Hellenistic success. In our typical Canadian version, Margaret Laurence's Jesus-of-the-stained-glass-window expiring "with absolutely no inconvenience" on what might "under other circumstances" have been a cross captures the spirit of the thing. The great problem with so much Christianity in our society — especially in its dominant Protestant forms — is that it has functioned as a dimension of the repressive psychology of the middle classes. It has perceived its rôle primarily not as a place of honest exposure to the problems, impasses, hostilities, alienation, despair, and sin of individuals and society, but rather as a place of answering and succour, a sanctuary from the night, a shelter from our "winter." Thus it has aligned itself in a rudimentary way with the official optimism of the other established institutions and agencies of society. It could not function as a forum for the confrontation with personal or social despair so long as it wanted to be part of that establishment. It had to affirm the fundamental values and goals of the society, and therefore it could not seriously entertain the dark side which was often aggravated by those very values and goals.

Authentic hope, I have insisted, emerges only where there has been and continues to be an honest facing of the condition which makes hope necessary. Real hope is only experienced under the conditions of sin, that is, as a redemptive possibility which engages despair. I regard this as an elementary principle of hope, demonstrable not only on theological and biblical grounds but on psychological and sociological grounds as well. I do not want to be heard to say that all forms of Christianity in our society have been indulging in shallow or false hope. But it would be less than realistic, I believe, if we did not admit that the most characteristic forms of our church life have presented us with the spectacle of an Easter Sunday in which there was very little of Good Friday.

Fifth — and partly as a consequence of the foregoing — much of the Christianity which has typified the Canadian ecclesiastical scene has been antiquarian and foreign. It has been addressed neither to our time nor to our place. It has not been indigenous to our own experience as a people. This has been demonstrated by many different things, including the fact that we have been notorious theological borrowers, as has been said previously. Even today we would rather borrow Liberation Theology or some other theme or slogan from beyond our own situation than to expose ourselves deeply and critically to our own darkness.

But our Christianity has not only been foreign, it has been antiquarian. That is, it has been largely addressed not to an age which experiences the anxiety of "meaninglessness and despair" (Tillich) but to other ages with other anxieties. As we have seen in connection with the discussion of sin, in a time when the characteristic hurt of humanity is despair, it is misleading to proclaim a gospel which was formulated for other times — for a time of mistrust like the era of the Reformation or a time of moralistic unlove like the era of the Victorians. We have said that the gospel must always be heard to speak to human distrust and human unlove. But it will not really reach these dimensions of the human condition today if it does not first reach and engage the human spirit that is in despair over the loss of meaning. I confess that I find very few Christians in the Canadian situation who impress me with the depths of their insight into the Age of Anxiety, Canadian style. For the most part, those who are not still beating the drum for a return to faith (the theological conservatives) are repeating the tedious-if-true message of theological liberalism that God loves us. Few of us seem to have explored sufficiently the contemporary Slough of Despond to begin imaginatively to address our society with a gospel of hope — genuine hope, not just the old optimism in some new and swinging disguise!

To make good the new image of the church which, here and there, we have begun to grasp, we must engage in an assessment of these and similar remnants of the old image of the church. It must be a more critical assessment than we have so far shown the inclination to undertake. Until we have identified God's judgment of our own past life forms and their continuing influence upon us, we shall not be in a position to become prophetically critical of our culture. Canada in crisis calls for a community of faith which, having opened itself to the "krisis which begins at the household of God" (I Peter 4:17), is neither afraid of human crises nor self-righteous in relation to those who are afraid.

7
The Pursuit of the Possible

The Argument

The most decisive thing in prophetic Christianity is its self-criticism. Submitting itself to the krisis of God the church is enabled to cast off the old forms and attachments which inhibit its full participation in the problems and possibilities of the historical moment. In Canada today a church freed from ethnic, economic, class, and other interests and identities could function as a forum of caring in the midst of a society in crisis.

Semper Reformanda

No one expects the church to be perfect — not, at any rate, people who know the New Testament. For one thing, a "perfect" church would hardly serve as a point of contact for the gospel in a quite imperfect world. Perfect churches, that is, churches which aim at what they imagine to be Christian perfection, regularly end as ghettos; they can hardly exist as "salt," "yeast," "seed," or "candle" *in* the world when they are so fearful of contamination *by* the world. About the church one has always to say what Luther said of the Christian individual: "At the same time justified and sinner" *(simul justus et peccator)*. The church is a community of sinners who know that they are sinners but who cling to the good news that they are nonetheless "accepted."

But (there is always a "but" in Christian theology!) the recognition that the church is not and cannot be perfect does not
mean that it can rest content with the status quo, with its ad-
mixture of obedience and disobedience, redemption and sin.
The grace which justifies us quite apart from our "works" also
grasps and tries to change us. Always we are beckoned by the
"new creaturehood" that is the gift of this grace; always the
Spirit of God struggles with our spirits to transform us — to
make us conform to the Christ whose body we are.

In the language of the Reformation, the church of Jesus Christ
is always in the state of reforming itself and being re-formed
(semper reformanda). Not just once in a while; not merely at
particular "high points" of its history, but always — *semper*! At
every period and in every place the church is called to submit
itself to the *krisis* of God — and therefore to engage in *criti*cism
of itself, in order that it may become who and what it is: Christ's
body. Its temptation is always to forfeit this identity for one that
is more acceptable to the world in which it finds itself — and to
the world *within* itself. Its temptation is also to rest content
with old forms of itself and expressions of its message which
have become superficially acceptable or at least predictable.
Humanly enough, the church resists the transformation that
the reforming Spirit of God constantly wills for it. It would like
to rest, to have the comfort of the familiar ways, the security of
old ideas, old relationships, old arrangements with society. But
it is called to follow a Lord who is out there, away ahead of it,
always moving toward the centre of the human crisis — as of old
the Christ preceded his reluctant disciples into Jerusalem, the
centre of the storm. It is called to be a people "on the move" —
in via, in transit, following this Lord, the Head of the body. So it
must cast aside everything that prevents its discipleship —
every restrictive attachment, every antiquarian longing, every
confining relationship. It must always be reforming itself.

This is not something incidental to the life of the church; it is
of its very essence. Traditionally the "marks" or criteria of the
true church have been discussed under the nomenclature of the
Nicene Creed — "one, holy, catholic, apostolic" (suggesting
unity, holiness, catholicity, apostolicity). But none of these

marks is a very satisfactory way of discerning the real character of Christianity unless, behind them, we see the earlier, biblical concept of a people of God whose message transcends its own being, whose Christ wrestles not only with the world but with itself. If there is anything unique about the Hebraic-Christian tradition, it is the awareness that it is itself continuously judged by the God to whom it bears witness. Its message is not only for the world "out there," it is also for the world "in there" — in its own life! "The superiority of Christianity lies in its witnessing against itself . . . in the name of the Christ."[55] Self-criticism is not an end-in-itself. But it is a necessary means to the end, namely, the end that Christ's body might really become what it is, might really approximate the new that it announces, might really pursue what is possible.

What is *possible*? Against every fatalized conception of the church it must be said: Some things really are possible. Knowing full well the lethargy, the resistance to change, the comfort of the old, the lack of courage and imagination, and all the other things which really are present in the life of the churches, prophetic faith nevertheless insists that possibilities are there, too. And even where they do not *seem* to be there, they *are* there — they will be provided; for God does not require of us more than he can make possible for us. Hope is the pursuit of the impossibly-possible; and if the church cannot risk the pain and the dangers of such an adventure with respect to its own life, it has no business encouraging the world to think of changing *its* course. Against every "Impossible!", every charge of "Sheer idealism!", every "What can one do?" the faith which is hope against despair insists, "There are possibilities!" No, perfection is not the aim. The aim is life.

Possibilities for the Church in Canada

There are possibilities awaiting the Christian community in Canada today that have not been sufficiently explored. One does not say that everything depends upon the church actualizing these possibilities — such an attitude has already been identified in the preceding chapter as Christian "triumphalism."

Nevertheless the life both of the church itself and of our country could be in some measure preserved and renewed if these possibilities were to become more consistently our real priorities.

As with every genuine expression of hope, the pursuit of these possibilities involves suffering. They cannot be taken up by us unless we let go of other possibilities to which we have been clinging for generations, even centuries. But suffering belongs to the life of all who would give birth to the new; it belongs indelibly to the "people of the cross." Besides, the old "possibilities" to which we are still trying to hold fast, such as the Christian imperialism discussed previously, have become the real *im*possibilities for the church in the post-Constantinian age. It should not be so hard for us to let them go, since in any case they are being taken from us.

The following discussion does not exhaust the possibilities that I see for a church in Canada which has become open to reformation. My intention is rather to provide specific elaboration of the *kinds* of possibilities I believe to be present for such a church.

(i)   *A Community of Dialogue:* We have thought of the events in French Canada within the past decades as constituting an "intimation of hope." We have also seen that what prevents this from becoming hope for Canada and not just for Québec is primarily an attitude on the part of anglophone Canada: instead of perceiving Québec's aspirations as a spur and pattern for the development of its own lost dreams, Anglo-Canada hears French Canadian remembering and hoping only as a menace. What if, in the midst of this state of misunderstanding and alienation, the church — in particular the anglophone church — were able sufficiently to disengage itself from its own ethnic, linguistic, and cultural identity at the sociological level to be perceived as a community of dialogue, not merely another representative of "them"?

There have been attempts along these lines. I was personally involved in one of them which was effective enough to make me believe that I am speaking here of a posture that is really possible. As a member of a committee on French-English relations struck by one of the courts of my church, I was asked to prepare a statement for presentation to the ecclesiastical body in question. I quote the statement here in order to offer a more concrete characterization of the posture to which I am referring as "community of dialogue."

We, the representatives of [name of church court], conscious of the opportunities for Christian work and witness opening to us at this time, wish to clarify our intention under God to serve Him and our fellow-citizens of Québec and Canada faithfully and with imagination. Addressing ourselves in particular to the anglophone community of Québec, and to [the church in question] . . .

1   *We affirm* that the Spirit of the God who acted decisively in Jesus our Lord for the liberation of mankind is ever at work in the world "to make and to keep human life human;

We lament, therefore, every form of cynicism which sees in political and other events of history nothing but the will of man and the clash of power with power.

2   *We affirm* that while no human deed, achievement or program should ever be identified unqualifiedly with the will of God, historical events which offer humanity a way into the future are never without a transcendent dimension;

We lament, for this reason, the tendency of some within the Christian churches to place God's providence so far above the historical flux as effectively to deny his love for the world.

3   *We affirm* the new sense of hope that has come to inspire our francophone fellow-citizens at this time; we give thanks for their openness to the future, and want to share in their enthusiasm for new possibilities of human community in this place;

We lament therefore the tendency of some of our anglophone brothers and sisters to give way to feelings of personal anxiety, resentment, and cultivated apathy, so that they miss the awareness of opportunities implicit in our present situation.

4   *We affirm* that Christians are called to involve them-

selves in the affairs of human communities, and without pride or quest for power to assume responsibility for society;

Thus *we lament* the retreat of many anglophones from this province, and the abdication of responsibility on the part of many who remain.

5   *We affirm* the manifest need for an anglophone community in Québec — "a new breed of anglophone" — which is committed to the good destiny of this province and its unique contribution to Canada;

We lament, therefore, the continuing spirit of narrowly racial, economic and other interests, which gives priority to self-preservation and to the fostering of ends which deny Christ's call to human solidarity.

6   *We affirm* that we are prepared to live in Québec as part of a minority; we intend to be a creative element within that minority, to support the vision of a better society as it inspires many of our political leaders, and to be vigilant for human dignity according to our Christian understanding of the nature of humanity;

We lament for this reason any remnant of false pride which may still keep us and our English-speaking compatriots from accepting the posture of such a minority, wishing instead to play a more dominant role.

7   *We affirm* that, in view of the grave dangers of a monolithic technocratic society on this Continent, it is essential for concerned Canadians actively to preserve the French language, culture, and heritage; and we recognize that in the face of such dangers government may need to resort to what may seem strong or artificial measures in order to achieve this goal.

Hence *we lament* the failure on the part of many anglophones in Québec and Canada to manifest a sympathetic comprehension of such measures, on the assumption that the preservation of the French heritage will occur as a matter of course.

8   *We affirm* that the present conflict is complex and multidimensional; it is not simply a struggle for the maintenance of French Canada but for our country as a distinct entity on this continent and a creative force in world affairs.

Therefore *we lament* the tendency of some simplistically to construe this as a struggle between French and English elements, and so to miss the larger issues.

9   Finally *we affirm* that the Church of Jesus Christ transcends racial, national, linguistic and other particularities; yet it is not indifferent to these, for it recognizes that human liberation is always being worked out in the specifics of daily existence.

So *we lament*, on the one hand, the failure of some Christians to rise above cultural and traditional loyalties to the higher loyalty of faith in the universal Lord, and, on the other hand, the assumption of some that Christian faith ought simply to ignore the particularities of nation, race, speech and culture.

In the confidence that we are not alone, that our God is present in these crises and uncertainties, and that many human beings of good will everywhere can identify themselves with the directions suggested in this Declaration, we commend it to all who care about our land, and especially to the household of faith.

This statement, which was presented under the title, "A Montréal Declaration," was endorsed by all but one member of the 10-member committee. The fact that it was tabled by the church court in question may seem to justify the charge that all such attempts at changing the church are idealistic. But that is by no means the end of the story of "A Montréal Declaration." In the first place, it has achieved a very wide circulation in church and society at large, including publication in national and international journals; and it is generally conceded that in this way it may have had a greater influence than if it had passed through the usual channels of ecclesiastical procedure. More important, it has been received by a significant number of

Christians and others in French Canada as an exception to the rule. Most anglophone statements, including those emanating from church groups, are open or cloaked demands for the rights of those making them. French Canadians were able to perceive in this statement something different, and thus to qualify their generalizations about the anglophone rejection of the aspirations of their society. The document and its reception suggest a model which, if pursued more vigorously, could make a considerable difference in the attitudes and events within Canada at the "turning point."

(ii) *Solidarity with the Oppressed:* It has been one of the focal points of the foregoing discussion that authentic hope only emerges in a dialogue with despair. The despair in question is not merely a theoretical despair, an attitude, a set of ideas. It is worked out very concretely within the life of our society. While it can be suppressed or repressed in the affluent, often it is raw and bleeding in the lives of the sensitive and the poor. In fact, the repression of this despair and its causes on the part of the affluent is possible only at the expense of these others, especially the poor, who do not have the wherewithal necessary for the pursuit of the way of forgetfulness and pleasure.

When we affirm that real hope only emerges out of a dialogue with despair, we are in that moment saying that such hope will not emerge for the church except insofar as it identifies itself with those who are the primary *victims* of societal despair. There are very good reasons why the prophets and apostles are always insisting upon the solidarity of the community of faith with the oppressed. For one thing, the forms of hope entertained by religious communities *not* in solidarity with the oppressed are often highly theoretical. Besides that, they frequently mask the aspirations of the powerful, whose freedom from anxiety is maintained at the expense of the less powerful and oppressed elements of the society.

If the church in Canada, in order to take up the possibility of being a community of dialogue in solidarity with the oppressed, must relinquish its traditional rôle as cultic spokesman for this or that ethnic-linguistic group, it must similarly relinquish its traditional ties with powerful economic and class interests.

This is a very painful process, for these ties are very firmly established. Their origins must be traced back at least as far as the establishment of the Christian religion under Constantine the Great, after which it became the church's habitual way to establish and sustain its ties with the powerful. It has devoted much of its energies through the ages to the maintenance of that solidarity. It has been careful not to offend its primary sponsor, and only rarely has it exercised a truly prophetic ministry vis a vis either the state or the ruling classes of the societies with which it has cohabited.

Thus to embrace a solidarity with the oppressed and poor elements of our society represents almost an about-face for historic Christianity. Yet it is possible. The possibility has been explored by many courageous people in the churches, some of them in high positions of leadership. Not only in their fraternity with indigenous peoples, unskilled labour, sexual minorities, ethnic minorities, the aged and ill, youth, and many other oppressed groups, but also in their confrontation of power-elements (big business, multinationals, military complexes), these persons and Christian minorities have given us evidence of what can be achieved in this area. The achievement should not be seen only in terms of actual deeds done and changes made — though these are not unimportant. The more significant achievement in terms of long-range influence has to do directly with delivering the churches from purely rhetorical, pietistic, and sentimental expressions of Christian hope and teaching us to think historically, contextually, and concretely. This is of lasting importance, for if the test of hope really is its capacity for standing up to the data of despair, then that means its capacity for making some kind of sense to those in whom the despair is keenest and most unrelieved. The reason why we must make greater and more consistent efforts to achieve solidarity with these latter, then, is not simply because they need us; it is also because we need them. Without them our hope is hollow and unreal.

(iii)   *Stewards of Nature:* We have regarded it as a sign of hope in Canadian society that there have emerged environmental and ecological groups, alternative energy movements, and similar minorities who protest the rape of nature by the dominant, technocratic culture. Like other causes embraced by our diverse protesting minority, this cause surely represents a possibility that Christians can pursue and in relation to which they can sometimes perform the services of the midwife.

Again this requires a certain about-face on the part of the church, and therefore to take up this possibility we must be prepared to undergo the pain of separating ourselves from our own past and from certain dimensions of our society which have continuing vested interests in maintaining the former arrangements. There are two kinds of priorities in our past which will have to be let go if we are to pick up this possibility. The first is related to what we have already seen about the church in relation to the poor. Because Christianity's establishment has always entailed confirmation of the values and pursuits of the powerful elements in each society, it quite naturally has lent its support to the technocratic empires of the West which began to emerge with the Renaissance, Enlightenment, and Industrial Revolution. Some of the Romantics (William Blake among them) tried to show that biblical faith did *not* in fact support the concept of the mastery of nature — that "dominion" (Genesis I) does not imply mastery but stewardship; for humanity is accountable to Another for its use and abuse of the natural universe. But Christianity was so tied to the apron strings of power that it could not and did not launch anything like a prophetic critique of the evolving industrial technological society. Thus for some ecologists and others,[56] precisely biblical faith is the ideational culprit behind the whole technocratic rape of nature! To reverse this reputation is extremely difficult, especially when in the main the church still raises so few questions about the technological society. We shall not be able to come to the aid of those who want to give Western man a new attitude towards his natural environment until we dissociate ourselves from this link with technocracy.

The second kind of priority we should have to revise in this connection is our habit of putting stewardship down to the bottom of our list of priorities! A very good case can be made for saying that the biblical metaphor of the steward (shepherd, keeper, etc.) belongs, not on the periphery of the gospel but at its very centre. Jesus' mission, it could be said, is to alter our human propensity towards either greedy mastery or slothful waste in relation to the earth and all its creatures, and to make us earth's stewards. This kind of phrasing of the gospel did not and does not appeal to a church which itself wants to play the game of mastery. So long as we are interested in pursuing the ways of imperial Christendom, we shall not be seen as midwives of the hope that humanity might at last find a new and gentler way of being "in" and "with" Mother Earth.

Yet it is possible! Enough of us have explored both the biblical roots of that gentler way and the prospects of implementing it here and now to realize that the Christian faith can walk that way, and can support others who take that path.[57]

Companions in the Night

One of the most important aspects of the despair which is at the heart of our Canadian crisis is, we have said, our refusal to acknowledge it. We insist on hanging onto an image of Canadian innocence, morality, and cheerfulness. The journalist Walter Stewart has attempted to dispel this image in his book, *But Not In Canada: Smug Canadian Myths Shattered by Harsh Reality*. At every point of our "smugness" (open door immigration, freedom, classlessness, law and order, racial tolerance, etc.) he brings evidence (and more) to shatter the myths. He concludes, rightly enough —

> I am not seeking to build a myth, but to offset one — the myth that we, of all peoples under the sun, have been magically endowed with qualities refused all others, especially those bastard Americans. It is a dangerous myth, because it blinds us to the reality we face in the coming decade.[58]

While Stewart's generalization may be true, neither he nor anyone else will be able to "offset" the dangerous effects of our "myth" by showing us all the ways in which it is daily disproven. We hold onto our myth because it is our blanket, our security blanket. Stewart is right in identifying this myth as being the element of greatest danger in our crisis. As a people, we must confront it honestly. But few people give up their security blankets, the comforting myths — even when they are becoming notoriously worn and frayed — until they can have some assurance, however tentative, that they can live without them. And they will not even be open to reflecting honestly on the threadbare condition of their myths if they have no sense of there being some meaning in the process of that honesty, some gain through the experience of that loss.

Christians have a story to tell, at the centre of which is a great and almost total darkness: the eclipse of meaning, the negation of the positive, the loss of hope, the experience of foresakeness and absurdity and death. That stands at the centre of our story: not the pretty scenes on the hills of Bethlehem and among the oxen (they were in reality no doubt far from pretty!); not the triumphant divinity / humanity of the Christ performing miracles and uttering marvellous wisdom and squelching his enemies (did it really happen so?); not even the glorious, risen, victorious Christ rising bodily into heaven (was it really so visible as that?) — none of these things, but rather: the cross. That is what biblical faith places at the centre of our story — not an isolation from the other parts of the story, but as the decisive element. For it puts God's own solidarity with us in our suffering, uncertainty, anxiety, alienation, death — in short, in our crises: the crisis of our humanity. And "if God is for us . . . ." then we may perhaps open ourselves to our crisis without ultimate fear — with fear, but not ultimate fear.

There lies in this story, with this centre, a most important possibility for Christianity as it lives in a context of human crisis. If it could learn how to tell this story in imaginative ways, and live it, it might here and there, now and then, give individuals and groups, caught in the web of events too big for them to contemplate, the courage to open themselves to the truth of their myth, to let go of their security blankets. Such a church could be a companion in the night to a society which is afraid of the dark.

But to become such a companion, the Christian church would have to undergo a serious theological self-examination. For we Christians have been telling our story as if there were no more night. We have preached the gospel as a success story — a tale in which all the negatives give way to positives, and all the anxiety gives way to joy, and all the darkness gives way to unimaginable light, and all the crisis-quality of existence gives way to ultimate peace-of-mind. Thus we have removed our story from the centre of human history, for the centre of human history is still a *critical* centre. The gospel as it is meant, and as we must now rethink it, points *toward* a "happy ending"; but an ending which humanity may experience only through going more deeply into that critical centre.

Perhaps a myth which helps Canadians *into* their crisis would be more to the point than one which assures them that the critical turning point was past and over long ago.

Conclusion

The Cross in Canada

At the end of his novel, *The Blue Mountains of China* (a poignant epic of the pilgrimage of the Mennonites from persecution in revolutionary Russia to prosperity in Canada), the Canadian novelist Rudi Wiebe has one of his characters carry a cross all the way across Canada during our centennial year. As a "Toronto paper" reports it:

> Calgary: While the canoe race and other centenary caravans move east, a young Mennonite walks along the Trans-Canada Highway going west. He is carrying a plain wooden cross. 'It's not really a centennial matter,' says John Reimer, 28, of Nabachler, Manitoba. 'I began it as a personal concern, a kind of walk of repentance you might say.[59]

What Rudi Wiebe means by this literary symbol I do not pretend to clarify. Symbols are always more profound than the words we use to explain them. But I think that I can sense, at an intuitive level of theological perception, the appropriateness of this symbol. It suits our society, which can no longer subsist on the highly "positive" symbols and myths that it inherited from the modern world view — the myths of progress and innocence, rationality and mastery, and light unimaginable. And it is appropriate for our church.

The cross that we modern, Western, Canadian Christians have retained (we could hardly get rid of it altogether) is the one that Margaret Laurence described. It is ornamental, ethereal, theoretical, liturgical, covered with Easter lilies, lacking in reality. In a word, it is empty. Jesus usually isn't even on it, or if he is, he's too often the kind of kingly Christ who is above it all or, like Laurence's "slightly effeminate travelling salesman," he is "expiring with absolutely no inconvenience" on what "might in other circumstances have been a cross."

In short, the cross we have raised on high, or kept suitably displayed beneath the "Christ the King" window on the altar, is no fit symbol for a society in crisis. For all that it can say is that we shouldn't take our human crises too seriously because they'll all come out all right in the end. But we *do* have to take the Canada crisis seriously! It is *not* a foregone conclusion that it will come out all right in the end. It is a real crisis, not just a flurry on the surface. Its outcome will depend in great measure upon us, our attitudes, our care or the lack of it.

Wiebe's cross is the one we have to explore and think about now — and carry! For, as he has his crossbearer put it —

> The church Jesus began is *us, living, everywhere,* a new society that sets all the old ideas of man living with other men on their heads, that looks so strange it is either the most stupid, foolish thing on earth, or it is so beyond man's usual thinking that it could only come as a revelation right from God. Jesus says in his society there is a new way for man to live:
>
> you show wisdom, by trusting people;
> you handle leadership, by serving;
> you handle offenders, by forgiving;
> you handle money, by sharing;
> you handle enemies, by loving;
> you handle violence, by suffering. [60]

Notes

1   *A Future Together: Observations and Recommendations* (Ottawa, Minister of Supply and Services Canada, 1979), pp. 3–7. [my italics]

2   I am told that in Chinese the word for *crisis* is made up of two other words: "danger" and "opportunity."

3   Deneau and Greenberg Publishers, 1979, p. 277.

4   *A Future Together, op.cit.*, p. 3.

5   Ibid., p. 37

6   George W. Brown, in Canadian History Association *Report*, 1944, p. 4.

7   Lest it be thought that this is said in a special way against *Québec* "regionalism" let me make it clear that (a) I have found this "regionalism" present in all six regions of Canada where I have lived, and (b) Quebec "nationalism" is if anything an *exception* to the rule, for of all Canadian regionalisms it is least dependent upon being "against," is most in possession of a *positive* foundation. (See Chapter V).

8   Something like Yvonne Deschamps' recent statement could be considered one pattern for this kind of caring: "an independent Quebec in a strong Canada."

9   "By ideology I understand a system of propositional truths independent of the situation, a superstructure no longer relevant to praxis, to the situation, to the real questions . . ." (Dorothee Sölle, *Political Theology* (Philadelphia: Fortress Press, 1971), p. 23.

10   Even the American-based Hudson Institute has made this one of its primary prescriptions for Canada's future; but it also notes that

Canada is prevented from playing this role on account of its relation to the U.S.A. (Marie-Josee Drouin and B. Bruce-Briggs, *Canada Has a Future* (Toronto: McClelland and Stewart, 1978), see pp. 24–25.

11   Christopher Lasch, *The Culture of Narcissism* (New York, W.W. Norton & Co., 1978).

12   As I have already noted in the Preface, this study began as lectures to the annual conference of Canadian Theological Students. The subject I was assigned was: "Sin and Hope in Canadian Society." I found it remarkable and insightful that the students' planning committee should have chosen precisely this language for its discussion of Canada today. It is somehow a corroboration of the appropriateness of this type of analysis at this particular time in Canadian history that a representative group of theological students from across the country should have worded their "theme" in just this way. It would not have been the wording chosen by *my* generation of theological students.

13   Ken Barth, *The Epistle to the Romans*, translated from the sixth edition by Edwyn C. Hoskyns (London: Oxford University Press, 1933).

14   Ibid., p. 142 (commenting on Romans 4:18).

15   Quoted in Alec Vidler, *Twentieth Century Defenders of the Faith* (London: S.C.M. Press, 1962), pp. 81–82.

16   *The Nature and Destiny of Man* (New York: Charles Scribner's Sons, 1953).

17   "Canada has been complacent about its future. Internal difficulties are now forcing the country to reassess its image of the future . . . ." (Herman Kahn, Introduction to *Canada Has A Future, op.cit.*, p. 25).

18   (Toronto: J.M. Dent & Sons [Canada], 1958), pp. 611–612.

19   (Toronto: McClelland and Stewart, 1965).

20   Ibid., p. 4.

21   Ibid.

22   Ibid., p. 6.

23   Eric Nicol & Peter Whalley (Edmonton: Hurtig, 1977).

24   For example the *Symons Report*, the first volume of which was released in March 1976 under the rather lofty title, *To Know Ourselves*, provides such provocative information as that, of more than 1400 courses offered in English departments in Canadian universities, only 8% dealt with Canadian literature. A similar "tremendous neglect of Canadian content" was found by the

Symons investigators in the social sciences and many other sub-
jects.

25 *Survival* (Toronto: House of Anansi, 1972).

26 Quoted in Don Fabun, ed., *The Dynamics of Change* (Englewood
Cliffs, N.J.: Prentice-Hall, 1968), p. 5.

27 James Laxer and Robert Laxer, *The Liberal Idea of Canada: Pierre
Trudeau and the Question of Canada's Survival* (Toronto: James
Lorimer & Co., 1977), p. 87.

28 See "Protest, Resistance, Search" in Chapter V.

29 Hugh MacLennan in his *Rivers of Canada* provides a poignant rationale for the flight to Nature. "The world of today is so different
from the one we knew before 1960 that we have all but forgotten
what the old world was like. A Canadian of 1945 could barely
recognize the Canada of now . . . . I found myself longing for something older and more permanent than human beings . . . . I wanted
to return to the rivers . . . ." (Toronto: Macmillan of Canada,
1974), pp. 7–8.

30 Elie Wiesel, *The Town Beyond the Wall*, trans. Stephen Becker
(New York: Holt, Rinehart and Winston, 1964), p. 176.

31 I Corinthians 13:13.

32 *Cf.* Dietrich Bonhoeffer, *The Cost of Discipleship* (London:
S.C.M. Press, 1959).

33 *Op. cit.*, see p. 37, also p. 229ff.

34 (New York: Alfred Knopf, 1978).

35 "The Right to Hope," *University of Chicago Magazine*
(November 1965).

36 See footnote 38.

37 *The Theology of Hope* (London: S.C.M. Press, 1967).

38 See for example, Marie-Claire Blais, *A Season in the Life of Emmanuel*, trans. Derek Coltman (New York: Grosset & Dunlap,
1969), and Andre Langevin, *Dust Over the City*, trans. J. Latrobe
and R. Gottlieb (Toronto: McClelland and Stewart, 1974).

39 (New York, Grove Press, 1968), p. 136.

40 See footnote 29.

41 *Technology and Empire* (Toronto: House of Anansi, 1969), p. 141.

42 (Toronto: Macmillan of Canada, Laurentian Library No. 1, 1967).

43 The title of one of the earliest and greatest films of a fellow-
northerner, Ingmar Bergman.

44 To put this into more technical theological language, they have all
participated in the attempt of contemporary faith to articulate a
meaningful "eschatology". Eschatology is a complex dimension

of Christian doctrine and cannot be easily or quickly defined; but in essence it asks precisely the question, What can we hope for? What is *ultimately* true about our human and Christian condition? What is the "end" towards which we are moving — "end" in the sense both of termination and of goal? What is the future we can expect? In contrast with earlier forms of eschatology, which tended towards "realized" expressions of hope, twentieth century theology has tended towards a more "futuristic" eschatology. That is, it has tended to be in the more definitive sense a theology of *hope* rather than of the realization of what is hoped for.

44[a] Ernest Becker, *The Birth and Death of Meaning* (New York: The Free Press: 1971), p. 198.

45 From an interview by James Quig, recorded in *Quest* 7, no. 1 (February-March 1978) under the title, "Quebec's Toughest Separatist Wants to Give You One Last Chance."

46 ". . . there is a possibility of a replay of the 1960s but perhaps even more vigorous and violent" (Drouin and Bruce-Briggs, *Canada Has A Future*, Op.cit.), p. 241.

47 *Theology of Culture* (New York: Oxford University Press, 1959), p. 40ff.

48 Martin Heidegger, *Discourse on Thinking* (New York: Harper & Row, 1966).

49 See footnote 38.

50 In all of the sub-groupings represented here we have indications — sometimes more, sometimes less direct — of broadly "political" activity in which there are intimations of hope. It would be possible to discuss the ecological and artistic dimensions of the protesting minority under the subheading, "political". But for the present I wish to use the term "political" in the narrower sense, meaning the possibility of a protesting form of activity occurring within the political structures of government itself.

51 See James Laxer and Robert Laxer, *The Liberal Idea of Canada*, Op.cit.

52 A figure like George Grant embodies this side of Canadian conservatism.

53 William Ophuls, *Ecology and the Politics of Scarcity*, (San Francisco: W.H. Freeman & Co., 1977), Preface, pp. ix-x.

54 (Toronto: McClelland & Stewart Ltd., New Canadian Library No. 3, 1974), p. 41.

55 Paul Tillich, *Perspectives on Nineteenth and Twentieth Century Protestant Theology* (New York: Harper & Row, 1967), p. 107.

56 See, for example, Lynn White Jr., "The Historical Roots of our Ecological Crisis" (Science, 155, (March 1967), p. 27ff.
57 I have developed these ideas further in a variety of writings, including an essay, "Man and Nature in the Modern West: A Revolution of Images," in Richard Allen, ed., *Man and Nature on the Prairies*, Canadian Plains Studies No. 6 (Regina, Canadian Plains Research Centre, University of Regina, 1976), p. 77ff.
58 (Toronto: The Macmillan Company of Canada, 1976), p. 283.
59 (Toronto: McClelland and Stewart Ltd., 1970 (New Canadian Library No. 108), p. 194.
60 Ibid., p. 215.